"Carroll takes us to the heart of the ancient prophetic message, focusing on justice, worship, and hope. The power of this book lies in the dialogue it creates between ancient and contemporary prophets. As readers we are constantly forced to consider the message of the prophets in light of present realities, and the response demanded echoes that of the prophets themselves: nothing short of repentance."

—**Mark J. Boda**, McMaster Divinity College

"In *The Lord Roars*, Daniel Carroll, easily one of our best scholars and teachers on the prophets, offers a concise and erudite— indeed, ideal—introduction to these all-important messengers of God. Carroll focuses on selected texts from Amos, Isaiah, and Micah while at the same time engaging everything from Don Quijote and Charles Dickens to immigration, the Inquisition, liberation theology, and much, much more. *The Prophetic Voice for Today*, indeed! And it has been fully recovered too, thanks to Carroll's masterful treatment."

—**Brent A. Strawn**, Duke University

"*The Lord Roars* offers a powerful call toward living a prophetically formed ethic grounded in the biblical prophets Amos, Isaiah, and Micah. This call is desperately needed in our fractured world. Carroll's unique lens of poetics and literary imagination offers a new way to encounter the prophets. Readers are empowered not only to read and learn but to respond responsibly. This means critiquing the structures of human arrogance and injustice in economic and sociopolitical dimensions, identifying the way worship and social responsibility are intertwined, and finding hope in the ashes through the prophetic vision of plenty, justice, and peace. The roar of the Lord is a call we all need to hear and heed."

—**Beth M. Stovell**, Ambrose Seminary

"Danny Carroll weds his deep engagement with literature and his lifelong attention to justice to recover prophetic imagination for the church. For those who no longer know the language of prophetic imagination, who doubt the Old Testament's authority on today's questions of justice, or who misappropriate the prophetic word on behalf of political agendas, Carroll opens the text's power to critique and to energize toward justice. With scholarly acumen and humility, this exploration is biting but also offers hope. In light of today's many pursuits of justice, this book provides a clarion call for the church to fire its imagination toward a justice that is truly grounded in the prophetic message, is lived out in the life of Christ, and is now passed on to the church. For anyone praying, speaking, or acting toward a vision of justice, this book is a must-read."

—**Lissa M. Wray Beal**, Providence Theological Seminary

"Carroll masterfully portrays the ancient prophetic imagination to contemporary readers through Isaiah, Amos, and Micah, providing a supremely relevant word concerning how prophetic literature must influence the ethical vision of God's people in God's world today. Carroll's book is an invaluable, biblically faithful resource for Christians who wish to embody a contemporary prophetic voice to push back against the ethical failures of the Christian church, speak out against injustice, and confront oppressive authorities and structures. Carroll provides a particularly timely and restorative message for modern communities that have seized, clung to, and identified with factional ideologies that engender impiety. This book is a must-read for those committed to reclaiming the prophetic voice by proclaiming the vision of the prophets."

—**Dominick S. Hernández**, Talbot School of Theology,
Biola University

THE
LORD
ROARS

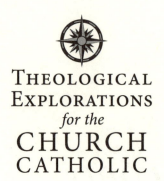

THEOLOGICAL
EXPLORATIONS
for the
CHURCH
CATHOLIC

THE
LORD
ROARS

Recovering the Prophetic Voice *for* Today

M. DANIEL CARROLL R.

Ⓑ
Baker Academic
a division of Baker Publishing Group
Grand Rapids, Michigan

Published by Baker Academic
a division of Baker Publishing Group
PO Box 6287, Grand Rapids, MI 49516-6287
www.bakeracademic.com

Printed in the United States of America

Library of Congress Cataloging-in-Publication Data
Names: Carroll R., M. Daniel, author.
Title: The Lord roars : recovering the prophetic voice for today / M. Daniel Carroll R.
Description: Grand Rapids, Michigan : Baker Academic, a division of Baker Publishing
    Group, [2022] | Series: Theological explorations for the church catholic | Includes
    bibliographical references and indexes.
Identifiers: LCCN 2021057338 | ISBN 9781540965080 (cloth) | ISBN 9781493436538
    (pdf) | ISBN 9781493436521 (ebook)
Subjects: LCSH: Bible. Prophets—Criticism, interpretation, etc. | Ethics in the Bible.
Classification: LCC BS1505.52 .C38 2022 | DDC 224/.06—dc23/eng/20220126
LC record available at https://lccn.loc.gov/2021057338

Unless otherwise indicated, Scripture quotations are from Alter, Robert. *The Hebrew Bible: A Translation with Commentary*. 3 vols. New York: Norton, 2018.

Scripture quotations labeled NIV are from THE HOLY BIBLE, NEW INTERNATIONAL VERSION®, NIV® Copyright © 1973, 1978, 1984, 2011 by Biblica, Inc.® Used by permission. All rights reserved worldwide.

Baker Publishing Group publications use paper produced from sustainable forestry practices and post-consumer waste whenever possible.

22   23   24   25   26   27   28   7   6   5   4   3   2   1

To the friends and colleagues
in Latin America, Great Britain, and the United States
who have spoken into this pilgrimage into the prophetic

Contents

Series Preface

Long before Brian McLaren began speaking about a "generous orthodoxy," John Wesley attempted to carry out his ministry and engage in theological conversations with what he called a "catholic spirit." Although he tried to remain "united by the tenderest and closest ties to one particular congregation"[1] (i.e., Anglicanism) all his life, he also made it clear that he was committed to the orthodox Christianity of the ancient creeds, and his library included books from a variety of theological traditions within the church catholic. We at Nazarene Theological Seminary (NTS) remain committed to the theological tradition associated with Wesley but, like Wesley himself, are very conscious of the generous gifts we have received from a variety of theological traditions. One specific place this happens in the ongoing life of our community is in the public lectures funded by the generosity of various donors. It is from those lectures that the contributions to this series arise.

1. John Wesley, *Sermon* 39, "Catholic Spirit," §III.4, in *Bicentennial Edition of the Works of John Wesley* (Nashville: Abingdon, 1985), 2:79–95. We know, however, that his public ties with Anglicanism were at some points in his life anything but tender and close.

The books in this series are expanded forms of public lectures presented at NTS as installments in two ongoing, endowed lectureships: the Earle Lectures on Biblical Literature and the Grider-Winget Lectures in Theology. The Earle Lecture series is named in honor of the first professor of New Testament at NTS, Ralph Earle. Initiated in 1949 with W. F. Albright for the purpose of "stimulating further research in biblical literature," this series has brought outstanding biblical scholars to NTS, including F. F. Bruce, I. Howard Marshall, Walter Brueggemann, and Richard Hays. The Grider-Winget Lecture series is named in honor of J. Kenneth Grider, longtime professor of theology at NTS, and in memory of Dr. Wilfred L. Winget, a student of Dr. Grider and the son of Mabel Fransen Winget, who founded the series. The lectureship was initiated in 1991 with Thomas Langford for the purpose of "bringing outstanding guest theologians to NTS." Presenters for this lectureship have included Theodore Runyon, Donald Bloesch, and Jürgen Moltmann.

The title of this monograph series indicates how we understand its character and purpose. First, even though the lectureships are geared toward biblical literature *and* systematic theology, we believe that the language of "theological explorations" is as appropriate to an engagement with Scripture as it is to an engagement with contemporary systematic theology. Though it is legitimate to approach at least some biblical texts with nontheological questions, we do not believe that doing so is to approach them *as Scripture*. Old and New Testament texts are not inert containers from which to draw theological insights; they are already witnesses to a serious theological engagement with particular historical, social, and political situations. Hence, biblical texts should be approached *on their own terms* through asking theological questions. Our intent, then, is that this series will be characterized by theological explorations from the fields of biblical studies and systematic theology.

Second, the word *explorations* is appropriate since we ask the lecturers to explore the cutting edge of their current interests and thinking. With the obvious time limitations of three public lectures, even their expanded versions will generally result not in long, detailed monographs but rather in shorter, suggestive treatments of a given topic—that is, explorations.

Finally, with the language of "the church catholic," we intend to convey our hope that these volumes should be *pro ecclesia* in the broadest sense—given by lecturers representing a variety of theological traditions for the benefit of the whole church of Jesus Christ. We at NTS have been generously gifted by those who fund these two lectureships. Our hope and prayer is that this series will become a generous gift to the church catholic, one means of equipping the people of God for participation in the *missio Dei*.

Andy Johnson
Lectures Coordinator
Nazarene Theological Seminary
Kansas City, Missouri

Preface

This book has its origins in the Earle Lectures on the Old Testament in October 2020 at the Nazarene Theological Seminary (NTS) in Kansas City, Missouri. The COVID-19 pandemic that was challenging the country in so many ways impacted these lectures in two ways. First, it made it impossible to present the lectures in person. Sadly, this prevented me from enjoying the gracious hospitality for which that institution is known. I did enjoy a glimpse of that warmth—although through Zoom—in my interactions with two of the biblical studies faculty, Andy Johnson and Jennifer Matheny, who took the lead for the event. Second, the virtual format meant that the lectures were delivered in one day, which resulted in two lectures instead of the usual three. The topics of those lectures form the basis of the first three chapters of this volume; what would have been my third lecture is reflected in the thrust of chapter 4.

The ethical demands of the prophetic literature have long captivated me. This enthrallment has its roots in my identity as half-Guatemalan (my mother was Guatemalan), which has marked my life and career. I spent time in Guatemala in my youth and later for many years as a professor at El Seminario Teológico Centroamericano in its capital city during the decades-long civil war. Questions about the responsibilities of government, the relationship between church and state in a country in the middle of armed conflict, and the nature of Christian mission in a context of violence and poverty drove me to the prophets for an orientation to those harsh realities of life. A year in Costa Rica, during which time I kept an eye on Sandinista Nicaragua next door and watched the Las Malvinas/ Falkland Islands conflict between Great Britain and Argentina from afar, and a stimulating two-and-a-half years in Sheffield for doctoral studies during Margaret Thatcher's final stint as prime minister contributed to that drive to engage the prophets, particularly the book of Amos. Since returning to teach in the United States, other issues have demanded attention: race, gender, and again, war. Involvement in immigration reform and Latino/a churches has occupied a lot of my time and concern in recent years. Through it all, my desire to glean a relevant word from the prophets has continued. It must!

The invitation to deliver the Earle Lectures provided a wonderful opportunity to organize my thoughts more formally and to put them to paper in this volume. For that, I am grateful to NTS and to Baker Academic. Jim Kinney, the executive vice president of Baker Academic and a friend, encouraged me to complete the writing of the manuscript. Jennifer Koenes, the project editor, was a pleasure to work with and proved to be a careful reader with insightful comments. I appreciate, too, the care taken by Auburn Powell, one of my doctoral students, in developing the indexes.

The title *The Lion Roars* alludes to that theme in Amos (1:2; 3:4, 8, 12) and hopefully communicates in some measure the seriousness and urgency of the prophetic word. This study is not intended to be exhaustive, and I have tried not to be overly technical. My hope is that it might encourage readers to engage anew those powerful spokespersons of ancient Israel in our time.

Many friends and colleagues, too many to name, have contributed to my journey into the prophetic. To all of them I owe a debt. May they appreciate this volume as an expression of gratitude and, Lord willing, as another step in learning how to better proclaim and live out the prophetic imagination.

Abbreviations

Bible Versions

CEB	Common English Bible
ESV	English Standard Version
HCSB	Holman Christian Standard Bible
MT	Masoretic Text
NASB	New American Standard Bible
NIV	New International Version
NRSV	New Revised Standard Version

General and Bibliographic

ANEM	Ancient Near Eastern Monographs
BBRSup	Bulletin for Biblical Research Supplements
BCE	Before the Common Era (equivalent to BC, "before Christ")
BibInt	Biblical Interpretation Series
ExAud	*Ex Auditu*
Int	Interpretation
JSOTSup	Journal for the Study of the Old Testament Supplement Series
LAI	Library of Ancient Israel
LHBOTS	Library of Hebrew Bible/Old Testament Studies
NICOT	New International Commentary on the Old Testament
NIDOTTE	*New International Dictionary of Old Testament Theology and Exegesis*. Edited by Willem A. VanGemeren. 5 vols. Grand Rapids: Zondervan, 1997.
NTS	Nazarene Theological Seminary
OBT	Overtures in Biblical Theology
RBS	Resources for Biblical Study
STI	Studies in Theological Interpretation

1

Reimagining Reality

The Power of the Prophetic Text

Parameters of This Study

There are several parameters that define this study. Perhaps it is best to begin by making clear what this volume is *not*. I refer to its *scope*. I make no pretense of offering a comprehensive survey of the ethics of the entire prophetic corpus.[1] The compass is more modest; I limit myself to three prophetic books: Isaiah, Amos, and Micah. I do not do so from the conviction that they somehow represent the high point of Israelite faith, as some nineteenth-century scholars claimed. They argued that these prophets were champions of an "ethical monotheism," free of the baggage of deadening ritual, which eventually evolved into what these scholars believed was the legalistic religion of Judaism.

1. For a broader treatment, see M. Daniel Carroll R., "Ethics," in *Dictionary of the Old Testament: Prophets*, ed. Mark J. Boda and J. Gordon McConville (Downers Grove, IL: InterVarsity, 2012), 185–93.

These texts do engage similar socioeconomic, political, and religious issues, but not as those scholars envisioned. These also are the three books that people interested in prophetic ethics tend to go to, so a closer look is appropriate. Since this book also is about *how* to read the prophets, the smaller sample size is more manageable.

Three methodological choices vis-à-vis the biblical text ground the study. First, each chapter discusses only *certain texts* in these books, a set of passages that exemplify the ethical thrust of this literature.[2] Second, the textual exposition is based on the *canonical form*. While some approaches to the ethics of the prophets work with hypothetical compositional histories,[3] this study opts for the text that we have in our Bibles. This is one of several alternatives available to scholars, but I choose it for a specific reason. My goal is to make the ethical potential of the biblical text accessible to the broader Christian community. To concentrate on theoretical stages of composition confines the biblical text to the academy.[4] The canonical form, on the other hand, is the Scripture of the Christian community.[5] This

2. R. W. L. Moberly uses this approach, which I find helpful for theological reflection. See his *Old Testament Theology: Reading the Hebrew Bible as Christian Scripture* (Grand Rapids: Baker Academic, 2013) and his *The God of the Old Testament: Encountering the Divine in Christian Scripture* (Grand Rapids: Baker Academic, 2020).

3. A recent sensitive, informed example is Mark G. Brett, *Political Trauma and Healing: Biblical Ethics for a Postcolonial World* (Grand Rapids: Eerdmans, 2016).

4. Scholarly critical matters regarding the composition of our three books are complex, especially for Isaiah. I am aware of these, but this volume engages these books as discrete prophetic books. I reference relevant background matters in the discussion and footnotes, but in line with the purpose of this volume, I do not engage composition debates. My focus is the ethical visions of the worlds within these three texts.

5. See Moberly, *God of the Old Testament*, 1–12; R. W. L. Moberly, *The Bible in a Disenchanted Age: The Enduring Possibility of Christian Faith*, Theological Explorations of the Church Catholic (Grand Rapids: Baker Academic, 2018); cf. Christopher R. Seitz, *Prophecy and Hermeneutics: Toward a New Introduction to the Prophets*, STI (Grand Rapids: Baker Academic, 2007); M. Daniel Carroll R., "Ethics and Old Testament Interpretation," in *Hearing the Old Testament: Listening for God's Address*, ed. C. Bartholomew and D. Beldman (Grand Rapids: Eerdmans, 2012), 210–20.

is the only text it knows and, in the community of faith's best moments, the one by which it lives and is shaped.

This conviction to engage the prophetic text as Christian Scripture leads to the third methodological decision. This book focuses on *formative, constructive contributions* that this prophetic literature can make to the ethical vision of the people of God in today's world. Not all agree that the prophets can, or should, fulfill that role. Cyril Rodd represents the voice of total rejection of the prophets for ethics. He believes that they simply were not as interested in such things as we think they were. Even if they had been, he believes, their views are unacceptable today. Rodd says, "Most students of the Old Testament see the prophets as at the heart of Old Testament ethics. This is strange. As I hope to show, ethics in our sense does not form a major part of their message. Moreover, their approach to preaching is in many ways utterly foreign to our views of the way ethics should be done."[6] And again:

> We would give no credence at all to a political speaker who declared that his criticism of some economic or social scandal came from God through a vision. We demand research before we take any action, and politicians often use this universal demand as an excuse to avoid implementing measures which they know will be unpopular or which entail a heavy cost financially. . . . The notion of divine punishment is equally alien. The prevalence of consequentialist ethics, coupled with the emphasis upon research into the causes of social evils and the possible consequences of actions that might be taken to relieve them, means that we retain the idea that what is done will have beneficial or harmful results. But this is not what the prophets are saying. They hold that Yahweh will intervene personally with direct action, and this we no longer believe.[7]

6. Cyril S. Rodd, *Glimpses of a Strange Land: Studies in Old Testament Ethics*, Old Testament Studies (London: Bloomsbury T&T Clark, 2001), 292.

7. Rodd, *Glimpses of a Strange Land*, 296.

Most who have questions about the prophets as an ethical resource do not react like Rodd, against this literature in toto, but instead against passages in which challenging matters, like divine violence, surface. Some detractors acknowledge the prophets' perennial value but also raise concerns. This book is not an apologetic designed to respond to these critiques. I approach the biblical text as a divine word for the Christian church, reading it with a hermeneutic of trust.[8] This does not mean that difficult matters are ignored. Some arise organically in the exposition and are handled briefly at appropriate junctures.

Longings for the "Prophetic"

It is not uncommon for someone to be described as a "prophetic voice" or for a movement or church to be called "prophetic." In these cases (as opposed to popular understandings of the prophetic as detailed predictions about the future or as a personal revelation from God), the label "prophetic" refers to a person or group who speaks out boldly against injustice and confronts oppressive authorities and structures.

If we limit our attention to the last century or so, examples of the prophetic in this sense are legion and are found across the theological spectrum. One can begin with the prominent spokesperson of the Social Gospel, Walter Rauschenbusch. Rauschenbusch assumed the validity of the nineteenth-century position regarding the ethical monotheism of the prophets while also believing that their ancient message was transcendent. Of them, he says, "The vivid Oriental imagery of the

8. In contrast, a hermeneutic of suspicion reads the text "against the grain" and resists its point of view and convictions when they appear to contradict today's ethical standards. For Isaiah, see, e.g., Andrew Davies, *Double Standards in Isaiah: Re-evaluating Prophetic Ethics and Divine Justice*, BibInt 46 (Leiden: Brill, 2000); Mark Gray, *Rhetoric and Social Justice in Isaiah*, LHBOTS 432 (New York: T&T Clark, 2006).

prophets must not give us the impression that injustice and corruption of that day were unique. It is impossible to make accurate comparisons of human misery, but it may well be that the conditions against which the moral sensibility of the prophets revolted could be equaled in any modern industrial center."[9]

A few decades later, ethicist and public theologian Reinhold Niebuhr turned to several Old Testament texts to describe what it meant to be a "true prophet" in his day (1 Kings 22; Jer. 23).[10] He also spoke of what he called "prophetic religion" and "prophetic Christianity," which properly diagnose the depth and pervasiveness of human social sin.[11] In the next chapter I return to Niebuhr's view of sin in relationship to our three prophetic books.

More recently, the prophetic label has been applied to protagonists of the civil rights movement, particularly Martin Luther King Jr., whose legacy continues to impact national life so many years after his assassination in 1968. Much of King's inspiration and that of other leaders came from the Old Testament prophetic tradition.[12] African American philosopher Cornel West argues for a "prophetic Christianity." In contradistinction to a faith detached from contextual realities, prophetic Christianity, he says, is characterized by a commitment to human dignity and social transformation. It is grounded in Christian praxis and, in his view, is appreciative of what he

9. Walter Rauschenbusch, *Christianity and the Social Crisis in the 21st Century*, ed. Paul Rauschenbusch (New York: HarperOne, 2007), 27–28. This volume was published originally in 1907.

10. Reinhold Niebuhr, "Four Hundred to One" and "The Test of True Prophecy," in *Beyond Tragedy: Essays on the Christian Interpretation of History* (Freeport, NY: Books for Libraries, 1971), 73–87 and 93–110, respectively. *Beyond Tragedy* originally was published in 1937. I am indebted to Jeremy Sabella for an orientation to Niebuhr.

11. Reinhold Niebuhr, *An Interpretation of Christian Ethics* (New York: Meridian, 1956). This volume first appeared in 1935.

12. See, e.g., David L. Chappell, *A Stone of Hope: Prophetic Religion and the Death of Jim Crow* (Chapel Hill: University of North Carolina Press, 2004), 44–86, 179–87, 307–12.

calls "progressive Marxism."[13] Additionally, because of its theological and political stance for justice within their communities and in the public square, especially in the past, the Black church has been called "prophetic."[14]

Latino scholar Robert Chao Romero presents a historical survey of prophetic voices and movements. Beginning with the colonial period in Latin America and continuing through to current voices of Latino/a theologies, he posits a line of champions of the praxis of justice from within the unique lived experience of their communities. Latino/a churches that continue in this tradition pursue *la misión integral* (holistic or integral mission), socially aware and committed to being spaces that respond to socioeconomic, political, and spiritual needs and speak into the public square. This is their prophetic task: "It is my contention that these many Latina/o Christian social justice pioneers form what may be called the Brown Church: a prophetic ecclesial community of Latinas/os that has contested racial and social injustice in Latin America and the United States for the past five hundred years."[15]

13. Cornel West, *Prophesy Deliverance: An Afro-American Revolutionary Christianity*, anniv. ed. (Louisville: Westminster John Knox, 2002), esp. 15–20, 95–127.

14. This label now is contested. Some see it as no longer applicable to the Black church more broadly. See, e.g., the critique of some trends in Marvin A. McMickle, *Where Have All the Prophets Gone? Reclaiming Prophetic Preaching in America* (Cleveland: Pilgrim, 2006). For internal debates about the nature and future of African American church life and mission, note Raphael G. Warnock, *The Divided Mind of the Black Church: Theology, Piety, and Public Witness* (New York: New York University Press, 2014); cf. Bruce L. Fields, "The Black Church (Prophetic) View," in *Five Views on the Church and Politics*, ed. Amy E. Black (Grand Rapids: Zondervan, 2015), 97–124.

15. Robert Chao Romero, *Brown Church: Five Centuries of Latina/o Social Justice, Theology, and Identity* (Downers Grove, IL: IVP Academic, 2020), 11; cf. Harold J. Recinos, *Good News from the Barrio: Prophetic Witness for the Church* (Louisville: Westminster John Knox, 2006); Oscar García-Johnson, *The Mestizo/a Community of the Spirit: A Postmodern Latino/a Ecclesiology*, Princeton Theological Monograph Series (Eugene, OR: Pickwick, 2009). As do certain US Latino/a theologians, Chao Romero connects with aspects of Latin American liberation theology and the concept of *misión integral* of key Latin American evangelical theologians of

Activist and theologian Jim Wallis has spoken of a "prophetic spirituality" and "prophetic politics" dedicated to constructive challenges that emerge from the biblical prophetic tradition and that are unbeholden to either of the primary political parties in the United States.[16] A recent collection of essays titled *Prophetic Evangelicals: Envisioning a Just and Peaceable Kingdom* revisits key theological themes and their current social relevance as an alternative to the longstanding evangelical tendency toward apolitical pietism or default agreement with the political Right.[17] The "prophets" tag can refer to religious people in the United States—those under the broad umbrella of Christianity or beyond—who advocate for what are deemed progressive sociopolitical positions.[18]

This prophetic perspective is not restricted to the United States. Latin American liberation theologians championed prophetic religious orders and community leaders during the years of revolutionary struggle in the second half of the twentieth century.[19] Jon Sobrino, a Jesuit who has taught for many years at the Universidad Centroamericana José Simeón Cañas (UCA) in San Salvador, characterizes Jesus's ministry with the

the Fraternidad Teológica Latinoamericana (FTL). Note, e.g., C. René Padilla, ed., *Raíces de un evangelio integral: Misión en perspectiva histórica* (Buenos Aires: Kairós, 2020). For more on the FTL, see chaps. 3 and 4 in this volume. US Latino/a theologies have some theological roots in Latin America, even as there are differences due to context.

16. E.g., Jim Wallis, *The Soul of Politics: A Practical and Prophetic Vision for Change* (New York: Orbis Books, 1994), 31–47; Wallis, *God's Politics: Why the Right Gets It Wrong and the Left Doesn't Get It* (New York: HarperCollins, 2005), 72–84.

17. Bruce Ellis Benson, Malinda Elizabeth Berry, and Peter Goodwin Heltzel, eds., *Prophetic Evangelicals: Envisioning a Just and Peaceable Kingdom*, Prophetic Christianity Series (Grand Rapids: Eerdmans, 2012).

18. Jack Jenkins, *American Prophets: The Religious Roots of Progressive Politics and the Ongoing Fight for the Soul of the Country* (New York: HarperOne, 2020).

19. Equipo Teólogos, Confederación Latinoamericana de Religiosos, *Tendencias proféticas de la vida religiosa en América Latina*, Colección CLAR 24 (Bogotá: Secretariado General de la CLAR, 1975); Enrique Dussel, *Ethics and Community*, trans. Robert R. Barr, Liberation and Theology 3 (Maryknoll, NY: Orbis Books, 1988), 88–98, 213–14, 227–28.

disenfranchised as "prophetic praxis."[20] Ignacio Ellacuría, also a professor at the UCA and one of the six Jesuits assassinated on that campus by the military in November 1989, defined the prophetic as the announcement of the sharp contrast between present realities and the fullness of God's kingdom. This message is utopian, but it is made concrete in historical praxis and liberating socioeconomic and political approximations to that ideal. The prophetic, writes Ellacuría, denounces oppressive social structures and actors as well as the complicity of the institutional church and its hierarchy in injustice.[21] Scores of Roman Catholic clergy (most famously Archbishop Óscar Romero of El Salvador), nuns, and lay leaders were killed by military dictatorships from the 1970s through the 1990s, embodying what some call "prophetic martyrdom."[22]

Halfway across the globe during the anti-apartheid era in South Africa, *The Kairos Document* contrasted prophetic theology with state and church theology.[23] More recently, in his work on Jeremiah, Congolese scholar Bungishabaku Katho asks, "How do we define a prophetic ministry today? Who is a prophet in Africa? How should the African church live out

20. Jon Sobrino, *Jesus the Liberator: A Historical-Theological View*, trans. Paul Burns and Francis McDonagh (Maryknoll, NY: Orbis Books, 1993), 160–79.

21. Ignacio Ellacuría, "Utopía y profetismo," in *Mysterium liberationis: Conceptos fundamentales de la teología de la liberación*, ed. Ignacio Ellacuría and Jon Sobrino, Colección Teología Latinoamericana 16 (San Salvador, El Salvador: UCA Editores, 1991), 1:393–442; J. Severino Croatto, *Exodus: A Hermeneutics of Freedom*, trans. Salvator Attanasio (Maryknoll, NY: Orbis Books, 1981), 39–47; cf. the entire issue of *Biblia y fe* 41 (1988), titled "Profetismo y sociedad: ¿Por qué está hoy el mundo tan necesitado de profetas?"

22. Edward T. Brett, "Prophetic Martyrdom in Modern Latin America," in *The Oxford Handbook of Latin American Christianity*, ed. David Thomas Orique, Susan Fitzpatrick-Behrends, and Virginia Garrard (New York: Oxford University Press, 2020), 237–55. A prominent example in Guatemala was Bishop Juan Girardi, who was assassinated on April 26, 1998, two days after delivering the Catholic Church's report in the national cathedral on the violence of the country's civil war.

23. Kairos Theologians, *The Kairos Document: Challenge to the Church; A Theological Comment on the Political Crisis in South Africa* (Grand Rapids: Eerdmans, 1986).

its prophetic role in the image of Jeremiah?"[24] Many in Africa falsely claim the prophetic mantle, Katho claims. What is needed is a courageous self-sacrificing stance for justice and peace that can envision a new Africa. Jacob Onyumbe Wenyi, another Congolese scholar, explores Nahum as a resource for the traumatized victims of that country's wars. The book's poetry, he believes, can evoke memories of experiences of war, giving victims the language to verbalize their suffering and to come to God for assurance and comfort as a first step toward imagining a different future.[25]

These examples, and there are many more, testify to the ongoing clamor around the world and across time for a relevant word from the Scripture that can orient God's people in settings of inequality and unrest. What might be a way forward toward utilizing the prophetic literature in our day? How can we make sense of its vision and appropriate these texts for our context?

The Turn to the Literary Imagination

There are several ways to handle the prophetic books as ethical resources. A common tack is to identify passages that mention the poor, widows, orphans, and strangers and those that use terms such as *oppression*, *justice*, *righteousness*, and *compassion* and then to correlate them with situations in contemporary life.

Others try to understand the targets of prophetic invective with some precision by reconstructing what may have been the material conditions that triggered prophetic anger. Using the social sciences, these scholars hypothesize that the exploitation in Israel and Judah arose, for instance, because of an early form

---

24. Bungishabaku Katho, *Reading Jeremiah in Africa: Biblical Essays in Sociopolitical Imagination* (Carlisle, UK: HippoBooks, 2021), 29.
25. Jacob Onyumbe Wenyi, *Piles of Slain, Heaps of Corpses: Reading Prophetic Poetry and Violence in African Context* (Eugene, OR: Cascade Books, 2021).

of rent capitalism, as an exploitative tributary form of production controlled by elites, or because of abuses within that patronage culture.[26] This research is insightful, but the biblical pictures of eighth-century life are inescapably tentative because of a lack of textual, epigraphic, and archaeological data. Prophetic texts also are notoriously vague on details. What they offer are largely impressionistic snapshots of injustice fueled by moral outrage, not socioeconomic precision. These studies, though, do underscore that the biblical invective was generated within gritty, unacceptable real-life settings.

Still others compare the ethical concerns of the biblical prophets with the prophetic material of other ancient cultures to ascertain what may have been unique to Israel's prophets. These efforts demonstrate the distinctive centrality and breadth of ethical concerns found in the Old Testament prophetic material.

Each of these treatments of prophetic ethics makes a contribution to the topic at hand. I propose, however, engaging these texts through a different lens, that of poetics and the literary imagination. What does such an approach entail? I start with two famous literary works that can illustrate the kind of reading I propose. The first is from my Latin American cultural background. I refer to the most famous work of literature in the Spanish language, a volume that some argue marked a new beginning in the development of literature; some even call this book the greatest work of fiction ever written. I refer, of course, to *El ingenioso hidalgo Don Quijote de la Mancha* (1605, 1615)[27] by Miguel de Cervantes Saavedra (1547–1616). The opening chapter famously begins with these words: "Somewhere in La Mancha, in a place whose name I do not care to remember, a gentleman lived not long ago, one of those who has a lance

---

26. For a survey of these hypotheses, see M. Daniel Carroll R., *The Book of Amos*, NICOT (Grand Rapids: Eerdmans, 2020), 15–26.

27. It was published originally in two parts.

and ancient shield on a shelf and keeps a skinny nag and a greyhound for racing."[28] Most know something of the saga of Don Quijote, even if only his encounter with the windmills. Schooled by his obsessive reading of medieval romantic tales of chivalry, "el Caballero de la Triste Figura" (the Knight of the Sad Countenance) believes that he is called to make right the injustices of his time. The adventures and conversations of this intrepid elderly man display great perceptiveness about the human condition and about the historical realities of Cervantes's sixteenth- and seventeenth-century Spain. The book was birthed in the midst of the Inquisition, and its author had suffered much—he had been crippled in battle, been held captive for five years by the Ottoman Empire, and was later unjustly imprisoned and impoverished. *Don Quijote de la Mancha* is an amusing yet shrewd satire that exposes both the cruel hypocrisy of Iberian socioeconomic, political, and religious life and the contradictory ideals on which that culture supposedly was built and that were giving way to the Enlightenment. The fictional world in Don Quijote's head, his actions, and his rambling soliloquies constantly challenge the other characters' interpretations of Spanish society. This juxtaposition of views suggests, then and now, that readers need to ask who in the novel perceives the world rightly, why, and how—that is, beyond the cultural facades and from the underside of society (the poor, women).[29] Without a doubt, this tragic madman is the one with the clearest and most honest vision.

28. Miguel de Cervantes, *Don Quixote*, trans. Edith Grossman (New York: HarperCollins, 2003), 19. The original Spanish reads, "En un lugar de la Mancha, de cuyo nombre no quiero acordarme, no ha mucho tiempo que vivía un hidalgo de los de lanza en astillero, adarga antigua, rocín flaco y galgo corredor." Miguel de Cervantes Saavedra, *El ingenioso hidalgo Don Quijote de la Mancha*, Edición Conmemorativa IV Centenario (Barcelona: Alberto Blecua, 2016), 25.

29. William Egginton, *The Man Who Invented Fiction: How Cervantes Ushered in the Modern World* (New York: Bloomsbury, 2016); Carlos Fuentes, "Cervantes, or the Critique of Reading," in *Myself with Others: Selected Essays* (New York: Farrar, Straus & Giroux, 1988), 49–71.

Don Quijote de la Mancha is more than an amusing story (although it certainly is that). There are lessons to be learned as we follow the quest of this knight-errant and his squire, Sancho Panza. Puerto Rican Old Testament scholar Samuel Pagán argues that the ideals and courage of its protagonist— "un tólogo" (a theologian), declares Sancho![30]—live on today in those who dream of and work for a better world on behalf of the vulnerable.[31] *Don Quijote*, Pagán says, offers ongoing theological and missional implications. I would add that its literary features are crucial for this task: the vivid scenes and descriptions, the lively characterizations, the beautiful rhythm of its Spanish diction, and the humor and sadness of the ridiculous. All of these are integral to this work effectively communicating an alternative view of the world that questions the one that its readers inhabit.

My second example comes from the outstanding English novelist of the nineteenth century, Charles Dickens (1812–70). His works are an extraordinary commentary on Victorian England, especially the sprawling city of London that at that time was exploding demographically and was experiencing the crushing poverty born of the Industrial Revolution. Dickens's novels (like his essays and speeches) are sharp, ironic, and occasionally comic depictions of the idiosyncrasies, violence, and loneliness of that context. His work was designed to entertain, but it is biting social exposé as well. In fact, throughout his career, much of Dickens's energy was dedicated to various social causes.[32]

---

30. Cervantes Saavedra, *El ingenioso Hidalgo Don Quijote de la Mancha*, 615. Proper Spanish would be "teólogo," but the mispronounced "tólogo" reflects Sancho's educational and cultural level.

31. Samuel Pagán, *Yo sé quién soy: Don Quijote para visionarios en el siglo 21* (Miami: Patmos, 2008).

32. This is a huge area of Dickens research. Note discussions and bibliographies, e.g., in Paul Schlicke, ed., *Oxford Reader's Companion to Dickens* (Oxford: Oxford University Press, 1999); Judith Flanders, *The Victorian City: Everyday Life in Dickens' London* (New York: St. Martin's Press, 2012).

Dickens's attention to detail was phenomenal. He itemized every aspect of each nook and cranny of urban and rural settings, the myriad sights and sounds of familial and public events, and the intricate particulars of his characters' countenances and clothing, even reproducing the vocabulary and accents of different social strata and parts of the country. These descriptions often are hyperbolic in their abnormalities, and Dickens's characters can be binary in an exaggerated sort of way. Seldom do readers question who is good and who is evil; the emotional reaction that Dickens seeks to engender is predictable. These colorful characters are brought to life with consummate literary skill and serve as caricatures of basic ethical types, especially those of low morals. Morality is always on display, unavoidably involving the heart and moral fiber of his readers. One biographer says that Dickens "was one of the greatest artists who ever chose to write in the English language."[33] But his was style with a purpose.

To illustrate these features I choose not one of his novels but a brief work that is well known in the English-speaking world: *A Christmas Carol*. Published in 1843 and the first of his five short Christmas books, *A Christmas Carol* would come to play an important part in the revival of the celebration of Christmas in mid-nineteenth-century England, and it eventually became a cultural mainstay of the holiday season. The mention of Scrooge (now a moniker for a greedy person), Tiny Tim, the Cratchit family, and the three ghosts of Christmas brings nods of ready recognition. What is rarely appreciated, however, is that this story is, in some measure, autobiographical. Scrooge's sister is "little Fan"; Dickens's older sister was Fanny. Some of the portrayal of Scrooge's unhappy childhood mirrors Dickens's own. The Cratchits live in Camden Town, the same area that Dickens did for a time in his boyhood. More

33. A. N. Wilson, *The Mystery of Charles Dickens* (New York: HarperCollins, 2020), 41.

relevant for our purposes, *A Christmas Carol* is "an attack on
the very conditions of the time"[34]—specifically, the callousness
of the comfortable, the financial vulnerability of the under-
employed working class, and the misery of poor children. The
impact of a report of the Children's Employment Commission
and Dickens's recent visit to what was then called a "Ragged
School" explains the appearance of the two children Ignorance
and Want with the Ghost of Christmas Present. In this story,
Dickens lionizes the compassionate and charitable heart (in
the reformation of Scrooge), which for Dickens represents the
essence of the Christian faith.[35] The social quandaries of a
few individuals and their resolution through the efforts of a
benevolent benefactor are constant themes in his novels.

As in the case of *Don Quijote*, *A Christmas Carol* can be
enjoyed for its plot and for its amazing literary qualities. This,
though, would be a diminished appreciation that misses the
passion that drives the aesthetics and its formative potential
in both works. Although from different contexts, *Don Quijote*
and *A Christmas Carol* demonstrate the enduring influence of
well-crafted literature, of what some call "classical" texts.[36] The
latent power of such literature has been examined extensively
in literary theory.[37]

34. Peter Ackroyd, *Introduction to Dickens* (New York: Ballentine, 1991), 93.

35. The nature of Dickens's Christian faith is debated. For positive assessments,
see Gary L. Colledge, *God and Charles Dickens: Recovering the Christian Voice of
a Classic Author* (Grand Rapids: Brazos, 2012); Gina Dalfonzo, ed., *The Gospel
in Dickens: Selections from His Works* (Walden, NY: Plough, 2020); Christine A.
Colón, "Finding Hope in the 'Radical Ordinary': Charles Dickens' Perspectives on
Christianity in *Bleak House* and *Little Dorritt*," *Literature Interpretation Theory*
32 (2021): 24–40.

36. Hans-Georg Gadamer, *Truth and Method* (New York: Continuum, 1975),
253–58 (cf. 258–74).

37. Note titles such as Wayne Booth, *The Company We Keep: An Ethics of Fiction*
(Berkeley: University of California Press, 1988); Martha Nussbaum, *Poetic Justice:
The Literary Imagination and Public Life* (Boston: Beacon, 1995). Of course, the
recognition of literature's power is not limited to the English language. For reflec-
tions on Latin American literature, see, e.g., Fuentes, *Myself with Others*; Roberto
González Echevarría, *The Voice of the Masters: Writing and Authority in Modern*

One author whom I have found to be helpful in this regard is Robert Coles, a medical doctor and emeritus professor at Harvard Medical School. For many years he taught a course called Literature of Social Reflection.[38] Coles explains how he used novels, short stories, and poetry to provoke moral sensitivity and empathy in students. In his books Coles takes his readers through that same kind of exercise with selected texts. These literary works portray ethical dilemmas of various kinds, the life of the disenfranchised, the travails of marginalized minorities, and more. He communicates that in reading, one is given the opportunity to respond to the moral imperatives that surface through the characters, plots, and verse. The worlds represented within these texts correspond at various levels to our own and can expand our horizons beyond the boundaries of our personal experience. Through vicarious continuities (and dissonance), they serve to disclose dimensions of human life heretofore unknown to the reader. This literature may expose ignorance and prejudices toward the Other from whom we are distant (by circumstance or by choice), that Other whom we do not see or may disdain in the internal mix of our fears, arrogance, and self-righteousness.

This intersection between literary works and readers does not occur only at a personal level. Because we are social creatures, literary works also can raise awareness and questions about aspects of the social imaginaries in which we are embedded, those systemic constructions of reality that we take as givens.[39] As these works draw us into their worlds, we are

---

Latin American Literature (Austin: University of Texas Press, 1985); Ariel Dorfman, Some Write to the Future: Essays on Contemporary Latin Fiction, trans. George Shivers with the author (Durham, NC: Duke University Press, 1991).

38. Robert Coles, The Call of Stories: Teaching and the Moral Imagination (Boston: Houghton Mifflin, 1989); Coles, Handing One Another Along: Literature and Social Reflection, ed. Trevor Hall and Vicki Kennedy (New York: Random House, 2010).

39. For social imaginaries, see Paul Ricoeur, "Imagination in Discourse and Action," in From Text to Action: Essays in Hermeneutics, vol. 2, trans. Kathleen

presented complex visions of the good life and of evil, and in the process of reading, we make (and learn to make) moral judgments about all sorts of things. Robert Alter is worth quoting here in full:

> The claim that I am making is a fairly modest one, which it seems to me is variously and abundantly confirmed by the evidence of five millennia or more of cultural artifacts: not that there is an immutable human nature but that there are certain lines of persistence that cross over from one era and from one culture to another. Much about the way we perceive ourselves and the world manifestly changes as society, language, ideology, and technology change; but we also continue to share much as creatures born of woman, begotten by man, raised with siblings, endowed with certain appetites, conscious of our own mortality, confronting nature from various locations in our culture. . . . The characters and life situations of the narratives of different eras speak to us not because they reflect a knowledge which never changes but because they express a set of enigmas with which we continue to wrestle.[40]

Said another way, the realist novel, poetry, and other genres have referential, or mimetic, power. Through reading, our understanding of the nature and meaning of life encounters diverse construals of human realities, some of which expose dimensions of personal, sociopolitical, economic, and religious life that have been unexamined or underexplored and that may need to be challenged and reoriented. Of course, this influence can be for good or for ill, so readers must mature; that is, they need to become better, more careful readers (What is it that I am reading? How is it impacting me?) and to grow in discernment

---

Blamey and John B. Thompson (Evanston, IL: Northwestern University Press, 1991), 181–87; Charles Taylor, *Modern Social Imaginaries* (Durham, NC: Duke University Press, 2004).

40. Robert Alter, *The Pleasures of Reading in an Ideological Age* (New York: Touchstone, 1989), 75–76.

and wisdom in the engagements of the literary imagination. "It is not enough to read widely," says Karen Swallow Prior. "One must also read well. One must read virtuously."[41] What makes for good reading and astute readers is a matter of dispute, but ideally, reading can be a school for the mind and heart—for our humanity.[42]

The Prophetic Imagination

The significance of the imagination, understood as the vision through which literature shapes how we understand and structure our world, has been explored by several theologians, most prominently perhaps by Garrett Green.

In *Imagining Theology*,[43] Green's primary foil is the sort of scientific mindset and worldview whose exclusivist explanation of the world dismisses the existence of God and the metaphysical claims of religion as incompatible with verifiable natural phenomena. To counter this perspective, which is actually a competing metaphysics, Green argues that the Christian faith embodies a distinctive framework for comprehending reality that spawns a different way of life. Ideally, Christians are shaped and oriented by the unique imaginative understanding of the world offered in the biblical text. They should embrace this lens from among the siren calls of other explanations that vie for our souls. To opt for one of the other options, Green says, means "choosing the wrong paradigm—of misimagining the world. The audacious claim of Christians is that the biblical

41. Karen Swallow Prior, *On Reading Well: Finding the Good Life through Great Books* (Grand Rapids: Brazos, 2018), 15.

42. In addition to the works already cited, see (though with different points of view) Robert Scholes, *Protocols of Reading* (New Haven: Yale University Press, 1989); Scholes, *The Crafty Reader* (New Haven: Yale University Press, 2001); Alan Jacobs, *The Pleasures of Reading in an Age of Distraction* (New York: Oxford University Press, 2011).

43. Garrett Green, *Imagining Theology: Encounters with God in Scripture, Interpretation, and Aesthetics* (Grand Rapids: Baker Academic, 2020).

writers rightly imagined the world, including its essential relation to God. . . . Christians live out that proof . . . by faithful imagination—that is, by living in the conviction that the
world envisioned in the Bible is the real world."[44] The Christian
imagination ultimately should be rooted, he says, in the Bible's
"imaginative integrity, the power of its images, poetry, narratives, myth, metaphor, and hyperbole."[45] In other words, as in
the cases of *Don Quijote* and *A Christmas Carol*, the Christian imagination is shaped by a text—specifically, the Scripture.
Texts can impact our orientation to life, but, as *Scripture*, the
Bible's work on Christian readers carries more weight and requires special attention. This book will concentrate on a slice
of the Old Testament canon, the prophets Amos, Isaiah, and
Micah.

Discussion of the literary imagination and the responsible
reading of prophetic texts must begin with Old Testament
scholar Walter Brueggemann. His book *The Prophetic Imagination* (published in 1978), as well as many of his publications
since then, provides the groundwork for what follows. In that
pioneering study, Brueggemann says, "The task of prophetic
ministry is to nurture, nourish, and evoke a consciousness and
perception alternative to the consciousness and perception of
the dominant culture around us."[46] This is "dangerous work,"
he says, "because it requires an epistemological break with
the totalizing assumed world of dominant imagination,"[47] that
world of unbridled individualistic consumption, imperial eco-

44. Green, *Imagining Theology*, 38.

45. Green, *Imagining Theology*, 71.

46. Walter Brueggemann, *The Prophetic Imagination*, 40th anniv. ed. (Minne-
apolis: Fortress, 2018), 3 (emphasis omitted); cf. Brueggemann, *Theology of the Old
Testament: Testimony, Dispute, Advocacy* (Minneapolis: Fortress, 1997), 622–49.
Note Ellen Davis's components of the "prophetic perspective" of "prophetic inter-
preters" in *Biblical Prophecy: Perspectives for Christian Theology, Discipleship, and
Ministry*, Int (Louisville: Westminster John Knox, 2014), 6–20.

47. Walter Brueggemann, *The Practice of Prophetic Imagination: Preaching an
Emancipating Word* (Minneapolis: Fortress, 2012), 39.

nomic ambition, and destructive national security that is assumed to be normal and worthy of unquestioned allegiance.

Brueggemann is, if anything, an impressive wordsmith, and the language he uses in these quotes speaks to the lively yet formidable challenge of prophetic texts. The goal was (and is) to challenge the people of God to reenvision their context and consequently reformulate their sociopolitical and economic attitudes and relationships. He calls the two central components of this mission "prophetic criticizing" and "prophetic energizing."

Prophetic criticizing requires confronting a culture's reigning, assumed narrative about what the world is and will be—what he calls the "royal consciousness"—along with the co-opted religious apparatus and theology that legitimate and celebrate it.[48] This critical function articulates the pain and fears of that reality's inequalities and works to persuade its audience (and readers) to free themselves of this dominant construal and visualize a different way of living in their world. The prophetic denunciation signals divine judgment on the status quo. This effort is fundamentally theological and necessarily literary—that is, this literature utilizes multiple images and a vigorous lexicon to engage those who hear (and read) these words. Unavoidably, this contrarian stance generates opposition from the sectors of society threatened by the prophetic message. In other words, communicating that message triggers an epistemological clash over how to envision the world, God's people, and God himself. Unsurprisingly, some prophets paid a steep price for their commission as divine spokespersons.

The second task, "prophetic energizing," entails offering hope of new possibilities beyond judgment, of a world no longer held in the grip of dehumanizing systems. In the Old

48. Although I am appreciative of Brueggemann's paradigm, I concur with others who disagree with his overly negative portrayal of the "royal consciousness" and his strong suspicions of Zion theology.

Testament prophets, this hope includes the expectation of a righteous king instead of a rebellious monarch, a just social life instead of corruption and exploitation, the peaceful rebuilding of ruined cities instead of incessant war, and abundant food and drink instead of want. Restoration to the land and a renewed social reality under God will follow the disassembling of the world as the people know it. Although concrete in its descriptions, this prophetic hope does not name that future redeemer or indicate when that new beginning will arrive, but it does make clear that the oppressive present and the imminent judgment are God's *penultimate* word—there is life beyond calamity. The prophetic imagination can carry the people of God through sorrow to the joy of a different tomorrow; it can help move them from lament to doxology.

How does the text speak beyond its own setting to involve readers today? The relocation of this textual world, as it were, into that of its readers is accomplished literarily and theologically. At least two literary features allow the text to bridge time and place. First, the targets of prophetic invective often are presented in vague terms. As we will see in the next chapter, those who harm the vulnerable or who make unwise political decisions often are not identified by name. They are an undefined "they" or unspecified men, women, or social groups or offices (such as elders, advisers, or priests). Sometimes they appear in woe oracles in the form of participles depicting certain actions ("woe to those who oppress"). It is what they *do*, not their explicit identity, that stands out. This archetypal nature of prophetic texts allows later audiences, like us, to associate individuals, groups, and systems from our own experience with what appears there. The indeterminacy of prophetic texts explains how they live on: the past is a paradigm for the present. A second literary feature that engages the reader is the direct address to readers with second-person plural verbs and pronouns. The constant use of *you* and *your* implicates them in the textual discourse. The text is speaking to *us—now*.

The reader is also drawn into the text theologically, and this in several ways. For example, our three prophetic books consistently present themselves as visions and as messages from God. This is communicated in the superscriptions (Amos 1:1; Isa. 1:1; Mic. 1:1), in the call narratives (Isa. 6; Amos 7:10–17), and by speech formulas such as "Thus says Yahweh" and "a saying of Yahweh." One must listen to what is being said because it comes from God. In addition, ancient Israel and Judah repeatedly are referred to as "my people." If readers claim to be members of the people of God, then this word is also for them.

Ultimately, the theological substratum of our three books is making a theological claim as to *what they are* (the very word of God) and a theo-ethical claim in *what they demand*. Readers who identify the God of Israel as their God must respond to this address. Responding to the text as a prophetic voice becomes an act of faithful obedience. This listening or reading must be *receptive* and *responsible*—responsible to God, to the community of faith, and to the context in which that community resides.

These texts aim to clarify what our social constructs are truly like, condemn the sins that permeate all of human reality, and call the people of God to repentance in every sphere of life. Prophetic books reprimand and warn, announcing deserved judgment while also offering a glimpse of another tomorrow for those who have eyes to see and ears to hear. Then and now, *receptivity* and *responsibility* are the necessary responses to these divine words. Prophetic texts do not countenance neutrality or detachment as options. Marginalized voices, from various liberation theologies to minority readings and social movements like those cited earlier in this chapter, rightly advocate for committed, situated readings and voice frustration at interpretations that sterilize prophetic demands.[49]

This textual appeal may challenge the sectors of the Christian church in which, to quote Brent Strawn's important study *The Old Testament Is Dying*, "the Old Testament has ceased to function in healthy ways in their lives as sacred, authoritative, canonical literature."[50] Using the creative theoretical framework of linguistics, he compares the state of biblical literacy and belief to a language system. Strawn explains that language determines in large measure the perception and construction of social reality. If Christians are not well versed in the language system that is the Old Testament and also doubt the legitimacy of that language's world, then the Old Testament will be silenced. He believes that currently we are witnessing the pidginization of biblical language (and biblical literacy) on the way to its creolization, which would mean the creation of a hybrid language and faith different from the original because of other influences. This change is accompanied by the loss of "native speakers" who know and live out that language. The result is the growing marginalization of the Old Testament. As the Old Testament and its perspective on reality are minimized in such churches, acquaintance with that divine word diminishes as well. What will happen to the Old Testament, he argues,

49. From a Latino/a perspective, see M. Daniel Carroll R., "Latino/Latina Biblical Interpretation," in *Scripture and Its Interpretation: An Ecumenical, Global Introduction to the Bible*, ed. M. Gorman (Grand Rapids: Baker Academic, 2017), 311–23; see a survey of approaches in Fernando F. Segovia, "Introduction: Approaching Latino/a Biblical Criticism; A Trajectory of Visions and Missions," in *Latino/a Biblical Hermeneutics: Problematics, Objectives, Strategies*, ed. Francisco Lozada Jr. and Fernando F. Segovia, Society of Biblical Literature Semeia Studies 68 (Atlanta: SBL Press, 2014), 1–39; and the more accessible Justo L. González, *Santa Biblia: The Bible through Hispanic Eyes* (Nashville: Abingdon, 1996). For African American approaches, see chap. 3, n. 27 below. There also are examples of Asian American, feminist, and other perspectives that could be listed.

50. Brent A. Strawn, *The Old Testament Is Dying: A Diagnosis and Recommended Treatment*, Theological Explorations for the Church Catholic (Grand Rapids: Baker Academic, 2017), 5.

will be akin to that pidginization and creolization process, in which the original language world eventually is ignored and replaced by something quite different. Even groups that hold to a more traditional view of Scripture are becoming increasingly biblically illiterate and often selectively choose texts in accord with ideologies based on other grounds. In these circles, biting prophetic texts can be ignored and the power of their eschatological passages missed.

If these biblical texts are not read carefully in order to receive what they offer, and if this lack of attention is coupled with a refusal to change one's political convictions or with suspicion about whether these texts are trustworthy (because they do not depict Yahweh as one thinks God should be), the prophetic voice can be reduced to a secular agenda in religious garb. In the end, that "prophetic word" will become superfluous, without substance beyond the vocabulary of a particular social agenda. This potential danger echoes the recent jeremiad (i.e., passionate prophetic indictment and lament)[51] in the history of American politics by Catholic legal scholar Cathleen Kaveny.[52] She demonstrates that today, with the loss of shared theological substance and vision, religious discourse in the public square that postures itself as prophetic has degenerated into vicious, self-righteous diatribe with no patience for humble and constructive civility and exchange.

Conclusion

The aspiration of this volume is to help readers discover a relevant prophetic voice, one that is faithful to the biblical text and that arises from, for, and with our contexts to address contemporary matters. The approach of the prophetic imagination

---

51. The term *jeremiad* refers to actions and emotions akin to the prophet Jeremiah.

52. Cathleen Kaveny, *Prophecy without Contempt: Religious Discourse in the Public Square* (Cambridge, MA: Harvard University Press, 2016).

is a fruitful way to read these prophetic books as a uniquely authoritative word for the Christian and the church today. As literature, these texts must be appreciated literarily because, simply put, the prophetic voice is found in their details.

Prophetic criticizing and energizing, to use Brueggemann's terms, nicely summarize the essence of what we will explore in Isaiah, Amos, and Micah. Chapter 2 tackles the first component: prophetic critique.

2

Prophetic Critique

Deconstructing the Unacceptable

A recent article in the *American Journal of Political Science* establishes that ideological commitments are more foundational than moral stances in determining political beliefs, which is contrary to what some might think.[1] That is, ideology is key for predicting moral intuitions, not vice versa.[2] If this truly is the case, then the challenge, even the necessity, of a prophetic voice becomes more urgent. How can the prophetic imagination foster a truly biblical prophetic vision in this kind of sociocultural environment? What does *prophetic* mean in that instance? How does it work?

1. Peter K. Hatemi, Charles Crabtree, and Kevin B. Smith, "Ideology Justifies Morality: Political Beliefs Predict Moral Foundations," *American Journal of Political Science* 63, no. 4 (2019): 788–806.

2. This article defines *ideology* as the political commitments and attitudes that frame perceptions of reality. For its various meanings, see Jonathan Dyck, "A Map of Ideology for Biblical Critics," in *Rethinking Contexts, Rereading Texts: Contributions from the Social Sciences to Biblical Interpretation*, ed. M. Daniel Carroll R., JSOTSup 299 (Sheffield: Sheffield Academic, 2000), 108–28.

As explained in the previous chapter, the prophetic literature presents an *alternative* vision of reality that we are calling the prophetic imagination. It reorients the various dimensions of human social life and provides a lens to apprehend sociopolitical and economic reality as it is in God's sight. This is done through literary structures and devices, vivid imagery, and lexical choices that can shock the reader.

This chapter and the next concentrate on the condemnatory element of the prophetic word, which is what most people think of when they hear the term *prophetic*. The harsh invective against wrongs of many kinds and at multiple levels—local, national, and international—is the topic of this chapter. The other interrelated target of prophetic polemic, the religious establishment and unacceptable rituals, is dealt with in chapter 3. In my discussions of the biblical texts, I follow the order of Amos, Isaiah, and then Micah.[3]

The Haughty Will Be Brought Low

The denunciation of injustice is everywhere in our three prophetic books. Amos, Isaiah, and Micah decry the cruel mistreatment of the poor (Amos 2:7; 8:4; Isa. 3:15; 32:6–7; Mic. 3:1–3), corruption in legal proceedings at the gates of the towns and cities (Amos 5:10, 12–13; Isa. 1:23; 5:23; 10:1–2; 59:3–8; Mic. 3:9–11; 7:2–3),[4] economic exploitation of the vulnerable

3. This is the putative historical order of their appearance in Israel (Amos) and Judah (Isaiah, Micah). As stated in chap. 1, for the purposes of this volume I am not engaging debates about the hypothetical composition histories of these three books. In addition, in my treatment of the prophetic text I will be citing English-language resources. Significant work on the sociopolitical relevance of these books has been done by Latin American scholars. Two stellar examples are Esteban Voth, Edesio Sánchez, and Marlon Wined, *Denuncias de ayer que incomodan hoy: El mensaje del profeta Miqueas* (Miami: Sociedades Bíblicas Unidas, 2008); Pablo R. Adiñach, *El Dios que está: Teología del Antiguo Testamento* (Estella, Spain: Verbo Divino, 2014), 205–84.

4. Gate complexes were the places for legal transactions and commercial dealings in ancient Israel. See Philip J. King and Lawrence E. Stager, *Life in Biblical Israel*, LAI (Louisville: Westminster John Knox, 2001), 234–36.

> For the house of Israel is the vineyard of the LORD
>   of Armies
> and the men of Judah are His delightful
>   planting.
> He hoped for justice, and, look, jaundice,
>   for righteousness, and, look, wretchedness.
>
> Isaiah 5:7

that includes the expropriation of their land (Amos 2:6; 5:11; 8:4–6; Isa. 3:14; 5:8–10; Mic. 2:1–2, 8–9; 6:10–12), exorbitant lifestyles in contexts of great need (Amos 2:8; 3:15; 4:1; 6:4–6; Isa. 3:16–24; 5:11–12, 22; 24:7–9; 28:3, 7–8), crooked market transactions (Amos 8:5; Mic. 6:10–11), and more (e.g., Amos 3:9–10; 5:7, 14–15, 24; 6:12; Isa. 1:15–17; 5:7; 30:12).

Complicating factors would have included unfair mechanisms of taxation, pressures of international trade, the impact of war and tribute, disease, environmental factors, and building projects of the crown motivated by necessity (such as administrative buildings, fortresses) and status (palaces, royal residences) that could require forced labor. Many of these wrongs were perpetrated by elites, but the prophets also have the entirety of Israel and Judah in view. All were guilty before Yahweh, but those most responsible for this reprehensible state of affairs included political leaders and administrators, well-to-do landowners, merchants, and unscrupulous priests and prophets (Amos 7:17; Isa. 28:7; 29:10; Mic. 3:5–6, 11).

In other words, injustice was both broad and particular in scope. It was broad in that it permeated every dimension of daily life in the Northern and Southern Kingdoms: social life, the marketplace, legal matters, the political arena, and religion. This pervasive evil was cultural and systemic, and it sustained power differentials within both nations. What was worse, individuals and the structures designated to ensure justice and the common good had failed and even facilitated these moral violations. It also is particular in that specific persons controlled and profited from these wrongs, whether through monetary gain or through greater prestige and privilege.

Yahweh, the Holy One of Israel, is a God who loves justice and whose rule is defined by righteousness (Isa. 5:7, 16; 28:17; 30:18; 33:22).[5] Justice is intrinsic to God's character, which explains the constant divine demand for justice; it is a good to be sought by all (e.g., Amos 5:14–15, 24; Isa. 56:1; Mic. 6:8). To twist it or deny it is an affront to God. Something deep in humanity, in both individuals and communities, motivates these sins. To this I now turn, performing a *prophetic diagnostic* of a fundamental root of injustice.

Amos, Isaiah, and Micah reveal that what lies at the heart of much cultural, sociopolitical, and economic sin is hubris, or excessive pride. This attitude of superiority and entitlement, often accompanied by a sense of indestructability, lies at the root of the exploitation of the vulnerable. Importantly, hubris is not limited to individuals or certain social groups. The prophets tell us that it also characterizes entire countries who believe, in modern terms, in national exceptionalism. This destructive vanity was notable in Israel's and Judah's leadership, especially their kings, even as it was present in the general population's understanding of Yahweh's support for the nation. God's people should have known better in light of their history and laws, and the prophets vociferously reminded them of their obligations. As the saying goes, arrogance breeds contempt; biblically, it also brings condemnation.

5. More couplings of justice and righteousness include Amos 5:7, 24; 6:12; Isa. 59:9, 14. For these two concepts, see Christopher J. H. Wright, *Old Testament Ethics for the People of God* (Downers Grove, IL: InterVarsity, 2004), 253–80; Nathan Bills, *A Theology of Justice in Exodus*, Siphrut 26 (University Park, PA: Eisenbrauns, 2020), 33–78; cf. Andrew T. Abernethy, *Discovering Isaiah: Content, Interpretation, Reception*, Discovering Biblical Texts (Grand Rapids: Eerdmans, 2021), 142–64.

Pride is a major scriptural theme, and in the history of Christian thought it is counted as one of the seven deadly sins.[6] Reinhold Niebuhr is exceptionally eloquent in highlighting the centrality of hubris in his analysis of mid-twentieth-century society. In several publications Niebuhr argues that humanity perversely ignores the limitations of its finitude; its original sin is the ambition to claim a status beyond its grasp. Humankind is capable of wonderful achievements but has this darker side too. Niebuhr explains that humans, made in the image of God, have the freedom to choose a different path but instead covet the stature of their Creator and the God of history. Tragically, but inevitably, this ambition plays itself out in the domination of others. Eventually this self-deceiving, destructive project is doomed to fail with devastating results.

Two biblical stories,[7] the fall in Genesis 3 (note particularly 3:5) and the Tower of Babel in Genesis 11, serve as Niebuhr's theological rationale.[8] These narratives, he says, teach that this inherent will to power is rebellion against God and makes humanity morally responsible for its actions. While Niebuhr applies this perspective to issues of his day, and even though there are numerous critiques of his thought, his discussions of human self-interest are insightful. Niebuhr stresses that, while human pretense manifests itself in interpersonal relationships, it especially plays out on

6. Note Rebecca Konyndyk DeYoung, *Glittering Vices: A New Look at the Seven Deadly Sins and Their Remedies*, 2nd ed. (Grand Rapids: Brazos, 2020), 41–66, 237–39. C. S. Lewis calls it "the great sin" and "the essential vice, the utmost evil" in *Mere Christianity*, rev. and amp. ed. (New York: HarperSanFrancisco, 2001), 121. See Lewis's discussion of pride on pp. 120–28.

7. Niebuhr calls them myths. By this he means that they are narratives that impart deep truths, not historical accounts. For an explanation of this understanding of the term *myth*, see J. W. Rogerson, "Myth in the Old Testament," in *Cultural Landscapes and the Bible: Collected Essays* (Sheffield: Beauchief Abbey, 2014), 654–67. Niebuhr's myths fit under Rogerson's "charter myths."

8. Reinhold Niebuhr, *An Interpretation of Christian Ethics* (New York: Meridian, 1956), 65–93; Niebuhr, *Beyond Tragedy: Essays on the Christian Interpretation of Tragedy* (New York: Scribner's Sons, 1937), 25–46; cf. Niebuhr, *The Nature and Destiny of Man: A Christian Interpretation* (Louisville: Westminster John Knox, 1996), which originally appeared in 1943.

a bigger stage, in societal tensions and in military and economic conflicts between nations.[9] Only "prophetic Christianity," he believes, is capable of recognizing this innate evil of humanity.

It is no coincidence that human conceit is highlighted in the prophets, and the Old Testament has an extensive lexicon related to pride. Most prominent are the four verbal roots *gā'â*, *gābah*, *zîd*, and *rûm* and their derivative nouns and adjectives.[10]

These terms are prominent in Isaiah 1–39, where they occasionally occur in clusters. For example, Isaiah 2 censures "the eyes of human haughtiness [*gabhût*]" and "righteousness [*rûm*]" (v. 11), "the proud [*gē'eh*] and lofty [*rûm*]" (v. 12), and "human haughtiness [*gabhût*]" and "loftiness [*rûm*]" (v. 17) in Judah.[11] In chapter 5, the phrase "the eyes of the haughty" reoccurs (v. 15) within a series of woes (vv. 8–23) that denounce those in ancient Judah who wickedly appropriate the property of others (vv. 8–10), participate in drunken feasts (vv. 11–12, 22), and pervert judicial proceedings for bribes (vv. 18, 20–21, 23). They brazenly challenge God to intervene in their activities, saying, "Let Him hurry, let Him hasten His deed, that we may see, and let the counsel of the Israel's Holy One draw near and come that we may see" (v. 19; cf. 28:15). Their self-importance renders them callous toward the less fortunate. They are self-indulgent and willfully blind to the ways of God.

In chapter 3, the ostentatiousness of wealthy women is depicted in a strikingly visual manner: they carry themselves pompously with a gaudy display of jewelry and fine clothes (vv. 16–24). This spectacle of the privileged follows on the characterization of the nation's leaders as those who have "ravaged" and

9. For an early discussion, see Reinhold Niebuhr, *Moral Man and Immoral Society: A Study in Ethics and Politics* (New York: Scribner's Sons, 1932).

10. The derivatives of *gā'â* are *gē'*, *gē'eh*, *ga'ăvâ*, *gā'ôn*, *gē'ût*; of *gābah*: *gābōah*, *gōbah*, *gabhût*; of *zîd*: *zādôn*, *zēd*; and of *rûm*: *rum*, *rûm*, *rōmâ*.

11. In this volume I use the recent translation by Robert Alter, because he attempts to capture the poetics and rhythms of the Hebrew text. *The Hebrew Bible*, vol. 2, *The Prophets: A Translation with Commentary* (New York: Norton, 2019).

> And humans are bowed low and man brought
> down,
> and the eyes of the haughty are brought down.
>
> Isaiah 5:15

"robbed" and who "crush" and "grind down" the poor (vv. 14–15). In other words, social injustice utilizes violence to achieve its ends.[12] Another shocking picture of self-absorbed leadership—now including the Northern Kingdom of Israel—appears in chapter 28 (cf. 9:8). Their arrogance is cited in verses 1 and 3 ("crown of pride" [gēʾût]), and their debauchery—including that of priests and prophets—is revealed in a stunning spectacle: they are impressively drunk, slumped over tables covered with vomit (28:1, 7–8; cf. 5:11–12, 22; 22:13; 24:7–11; 56:10–12).

One civil servant in Judah is singled out by name: Shebna, the steward of the palace in Jerusalem (22:15–19). He is mocked for pretentiously carving out a grave for himself in the cliff opposite the city of David, on the Silwan slope of the Kidron Valley. Burial practices were important culturally at that time, and this tomb would have been a public demonstration of Shebna's status.[13] Yahweh lampoons him as the "mighty man," whom he will grab, roll up in a ball, and throw away into a faraway land,[14] where his self-importance can save neither his life nor his goods. Demotion and shame are his future.

12. As in the case of pride, the Old Testament has an extensive vocabulary for the poor and oppressed and for the violence of oppressive social practices. See Elsa Tamez, *Bible of the Oppressed*, trans. M. J. O'Connell (Maryknoll, NY: Orbis Books, 1982); Thomas D. Hanks, *God So Loved the Third World: The Bible, the Reformation and Liberation Theologies* (Maryknoll, NY: Orbis Books, 1983), 3–25.

13. Elizabeth Bloch-Smith, "Death and Burial in Eighth-Century Judah," in *Archaeology and History of Eighth-Century Judah*, ed. Z. I. Farber and J. L. Wright, ANEM 23 (Atlanta: SBL Press, 2018), 365–78.

14. Alter endorses the emendation in 22:17 of *geber* ("mighty man") to *beged* ("garment") and translates *ṣnp* in v. 18 as "wind around," rendering, "The LORD is

The same soulless disdain of the poor is attacked in Amos and Micah. In Amos 2, those of status sell those in financial straits into debt slavery (v. 6), and they "trample the head of the needy" and "pervert the way of the poor" (v. 7). In 4:1, wealthy women (who are lampooned as "cows of Bashan") "exploit" and "crush" the poor, even as they clamor for more drink. In chapter 6 those sprawled out on beds of ivory and comfortable couches eat the best meat (a rare delicacy for the general population),[15] drink wine (cf. 2:8), and anoint themselves with the finest oil. They are oblivious to "Joseph's disaster," the suffering of the less fortunate all around them (6:4–7).[16] In chapter 8, merchants "trample the needy" and destroy "the poor of the land" with their scheming (v. 4); they manipulate the marketplace with dishonest scales and sell grain mixed with chaff (v. 6b); and they "buy the indigent" (v. 6a), likely those of 2:6 who were forced to sell themselves or family members to pay off debt. The vulnerable are helpless and expendable, while the well-placed believe that they are untouchable (9:10).

In Micah 2 the haughty "walk with high [*rômâ*] heads" (v. 3) and covet the property of others. They plot on their beds to seize land from others because they are in a position to do so (v. 1). In that world, privilege and might made right. Truly, it was an evil time (v. 3; cf. Amos 5:13). Micah 3 graphically portrays the deplorable injustice perpetuated against the vulnerable by the socially powerful. These are people

---

about to shake you as one shakes a garment, and wrap you around, He shall surely wind you round like a turban away to a spacious land." For the translation assumed here, see other English versions (e.g., NRSV, NIV, ESV).

15. The population was largely made up of peasant farmers for whom animals were key to survival: oxen for plowing, sheep for wool, and goats for milk. Killing an animal to eat would have been only for special occasions. See Cynthia Shafer-Elliott, "'He Shall Eat Curds and Honey' (Isa 7:15): Food and Feasting in Late Eighth-Century Judah," in Farber and Wright, *Archaeology and History of Eighth-Century Judah*, 279–98.

16. Amos 6:3–6 likely describes the excesses of a *marzēaḥ* feast, which possibly was a funerary banquet of the wealthy. See M. Daniel Carroll R., *The Book of Amos*, NICOT (Grand Rapids: Eerdmans, 2020), 369–78.

> who flay their [the vulnerable's] skin from them
>   and their flesh from their bones.
> Who devour My [God's] people's flesh
>   and strip their skin from them
>   and crack open their bones.
> And they cut it like flesh in the pot
>   and like meat in the cauldron. (vv. 2–3)

These prominent individuals and groups (political leaders, chieftains, priests, prophets, and diviners; vv. 1, 5–7) hate good and love evil (v. 2; cf. Amos 5:15; Isa. 5:20). Judah's rulers "despise justice and everything straight they twist"; they "build Zion with bloodshed and Jerusalem with wickedness" (Mic. 3:9–10). Everyone can be bought for a price (v. 11). Contempt, collusion, and cruelty poison the social fabric; condemnable character drives the injustice. These prophets do not record the cries of those who suffered these injustices, as do other books (e.g., Exod. 2:23–25 and many psalms), but they leave no doubt that they speak out on behalf of those who suffer and that Yahweh will act.

The prophetic exposé of Israel's and Judah's arrogance extends from the socioeconomic to the political. This is most clear in Isaiah, which provides glimpses of policy decisions in Judah made by King Ahaz in 734 BCE (chaps. 7–8) and by Hezekiah in 715–711 BCE (chap. 20) and 701 BCE (chaps. 21–23; 28–33; 36–39) during times of Assyrian threat.[17] Ahaz spurns the prophet's wide-open offer to ask for a sign of divine help (7:10–17), having already made arrangements for Judah to become Assyria's vassal (cf. 2 Kings 16:5–18). To save his throne, Ahaz has mortgaged his nation's future to a brutal empire.

---

17. See M. Daniel Carroll R., "Impulses toward Peace in a Country at War: The Book of Isaiah between Realism and Hope," in *War in the Bible and Terrorism in the Twenty-First Century*, ed. Richard S. Hess and Elmer A. Martens, BBRSup 2 (Winona Lake, IN: Eisenbrauns, 2008), 59–78.

Decades later in 701, Hezekiah and his advisers await the arrival of the Assyrian armies. They have made the ill-advised decision to participate in a coalition of smaller states against the empire and have sought Egypt's help. Judah will soon suffer Assyria's wrath. In withering fashion, Isaiah condemns Judah's leaders, who cannot discern the times (28:14, 22–28): they are "perverse," oppressors and mockers (29:16, 20); "they are drunk and not from wine, stagger, and not from strong drink" (29:9), stumbling into this dreadful foreign policy. Judah's leaders have not sought Yahweh, who "is wondrous in counsel," but instead have devised their own schemes (28:29; cf. 30:1–5; 31:1–3).

Having forgotten how a decade before (711 BCE) the nation had followed the prophet's instructions not to join a similar coalition and had been spared defeat, these politicians now advocate that disastrous strategy. This choice, especially the partnership with Egypt, is not a lifeline but a pact with death (28:15). Soon they would be "crushed" by the empire and live the "horror" of military devastation (28:18–19). This foolish policy decision based on calculations of *Realpolitik* and conceived in secret, where they thought God could not see (29:15; 30:10), will bring the nation down (29:4) in "shame" and "disgrace" (30:2–5). The preparations that have been made to buttress Jerusalem's defenses against the Assyrians would not succeed (cf. 2 Chon. 32:2–8). Devised in self-deceiving rebellion, these plans have secured the nation's defeat.

The book of Amos parodies Israel's military pretense in its own literary style.[18] The nation celebrates its victory at Lo-Dabar and its might in taking Karnaim (6:13). This line is satirical genius. Lo-Dabar means "No-Thing." That is, Israel

---

18. Parody of the military is a key feature of the genre of the dictator novel in Latin America. See M. Daniel Carroll R., "The Prophetic Text and the Literature of Dissent in Latin America: Amos, García Márquez, and Cabrera Infante Dismantle Militarism," *Biblical Interpretation* 4, no. 1 (1996): 76–100.

is rejoicing winning at Nothing! The conflicts at its borders
(1:3–15; cf. 4:10) are a harbinger of imminent comprehensive
military humiliation. In that day, Israel's troops will flee naked
(2:14–16). Seven kinds of soldiers are listed—Israel will experience perfect defeat. The prophet announces that Israel will
fall to an unnamed enemy (3:11), who will oppress the country
from border to border (6:14). Israel's boasting cannot prevent
the destruction of its fortresses or the tremendous loss of life
in the war looming on the horizon (3:11; 5:1–3, 16–17; 6:9–11)
and the deportation that will follow in its aftermath (4:2–3;
5:27; 7:11, 17). In fact, the walls of Israel's fortresses are like
tin (7:7–8).[19] The nation believes that these walls are as stout
as iron, but in reality they are weak and cannot keep the enemy
out. The nation, which is so confident in its economic status and
military strength, is truly nothing; Israel is so "small" (7:2, 5).

Misdirected arrogance is evident as well in the posturing of
the empires that invaded Judah and Israel. Assyria was a terrify-
ing conqueror. Its cruelty was unparalleled in the ancient world
and was integral to imperial propaganda, both inscriptional
and monumental.[20] For decades Assyria's unstoppable armies
marched across the Fertile Crescent and into the Levant, and
the conviction of its invincibility grew. Through Isaiah, however, Yahweh asserts that the Assyrian king and his hosts are
nothing more than instruments in a divine plan (7:17–20; 8:5–8;
10:5–6; cf. 14:24–27). Success had bred a mistaken confidence
in the empire's might. Their king boasts, "Through the power
of my hand I have done it, and through my wisdom, for I was

19. I translate the Hebrew term *'ănāk* as "tin" instead of the usual "plumb line."
For a discussion, see Carroll R., *Book of Amos*, 409–13.

20. Theodore J. Lewis, "'You Have Heard What the Kings of Assyria Have Done':
Disarmament Rhetoric of Intimidation," in *Isaiah's Vision of Peace in Biblical and
Modern International Relations: Swords into Plowshares*, ed. Raymond Cohan and
Raymond Westbrook (New York: Palgrave Macmillan, 2008), 75–100; Charlie Trimm,
Fighting for the King and the Gods: A Survey of Warfare in the Ancient Near East,
Resources for Biblical Study 88 (Atlanta: SBL Press, 2017), 314–16, 334–42, 355–64,
373–77, 385–88.

discerning" (10:13). The truth, however, is that Yahweh will "reckon with the fruit of the swollen heart of Assyria's king and with the grandeur of his haughty [*rûm*] gaze" (10:12). Comparing the Assyrians to trees, the prophet announces that this forest will be cut down (10:15–19); its lofty branches and tall trees will be brought low (10:33–34).[21] Several other passages in Isaiah use Assyrian imperial motifs and turn them on their head. It is Yahweh, the God of Judah, that small country on the empire's periphery, and not the powerful king of Assyria, who rules history and the nations.[22]

The Rabshakeh, the official in charge of negotiations during the siege of Jerusalem in 701 BCE, verbalizes the Assyrian pride (Isa. 36:4–21). With the people watching from the city wall, the Rabshakeh broadcasts—in Hebrew no less (v. 11)![23]—that he has come in the name of Sennacherib, "the great king, the king of Assyria" (vv. 4, 13). He ridicules Judah's objects of "trust."[24] He begins by shouting to those on the wall, "What is this great trust in which you place trust?" (v. 4). It is useless to depend on traitorous Egypt for military aid, the Rabshakeh says. He argues, too, that there is reason to believe that the nation's losses in the war up to this point have been because Yahweh is angry

21. Trees were a metaphor for kings and countries in the ancient world. See William R. Osborne, *Trees and Kings: A Comparative Analysis of Tree Imagery in Israel's Prophetic Tradition and the Ancient Near East*, BBRSup 18 (University Park, PA: Eisenbrauns, 2018). Shawn Zelig Aster suggests that this is a reversal of Assyrian imagery, a tradition in which a king proves his worth by embarking on a heroic journey to cut down trees, a symbol of conquest. Here it is the Assyrian king who is cut down (*Reflections of Empire in Isaiah 1–39: Responses to Assyrian Ideology*, ANEM 19 [Atlanta: SBL Press, 2017], 231–34).

22. Aster, *Reflections of Empire*; Matthew J. Lynch, *First Isaiah and the Disappearance of the Gods*, Critical Studies in the Hebrew Bible 12 (University Park, PA: Eisenbrauns, 2021), 61–75.

23. The Rabshakeh may have been a descendant of (or even one of) those taken from Israel in 722. (There is evidence of an Israelite chariot corps being incorporated into the Assyrian army.) This might explain how an Assyrian could speak Hebrew and allude to Israel's traditions (Isa. 36:11–13, 16–17). It also was not uncommon for the Assyrians to have interpreters on their staff.

24. The verb *bāṭaḥ* ("trust") and its derivative noun *biṭṭāḥôn* are key to his speech.

> Look, the Master, LORD of Armies,
>   hacks away at the treetops with an axe,
>   and the lofty in stature are cut down
>   and the tall ones brought low.
>
> Isaiah 10:33

at Hezekiah (vv. 5–7). Has not Hezekiah banned all the high places? No god would accept the removal of worship centers! How could they trust Yahweh anyway? Thus far, no god of any nation has been able to stop the imperial onslaught. Yahweh has not been able to save the other cities of Judah (v. 1). Only the capital city remains, and it is surrounded. There is no hope; the best option is to surrender (vv. 15–20; cf. 37:8–13). But in a dramatic reversal of fortune, the Assyrians experienced the wrath of God. They withdrew from Jerusalem,[25] and Sennacherib was assassinated soon after (37:36–38).

The focus of Isaiah 13–14 shifts to another ancient power, Babylon. Yahweh announces judgment on the empire's evil that will "put an end to the pride [*gā'ôn*] of the arrogant [*zēdîm*], [and] bring low the overweening [*ga'ăvâ*] of tyrants" (13:11). "Babylon," Yahweh proclaims, "splendor of kingdoms, the glorious pride [*gā'ôn*] of Chaldeans," will be overthrown like Sodom and Gomorrah (13:19). The grand king of Babylon, who once made the kingdoms of the earth tremble, will be brought down to the grave, to the shock of the other dead kings. His majesty will be of no consequence in the pit, where his corpse will be covered with maggots (14:9–12). This proud king, who foolishly aspired to a throne in the heavens, will be humiliated and slaughtered along with his sons (14:13–21).

25. For the Assyrian account, see the Annals of Sennacherib (William W. Hallo and K. Lawson Younger Jr., eds., *The Context of Scripture*, 4 vols. [Leiden: Brill, 1997–2018], 2:302–3).

Isaiah makes plain that hubris is the purview not only of great nations; it resides in the heart of all peoples. Of Moab, that small country on the other side of the Dead Sea, the prophet says, "We have heard of Moab's pride [gā'ôn], so very proud [gē'], his pride [ga'ăvâ] and his proud [gā'ôn] anger" (16:6). Yahweh of Hosts also decrees "to profane the pride [gā'ôn] of all splendor" of the Phoenician city-states of Tyre and Sidon and "to debase all notables of the land" (23:9). We are not told the basis of Moab's arrogance, but Tyre's is the subject of Ezekiel 26–28. Those chapters tell us that Tyre's pride resided in its maritime success and the wealth accumulated through wide-ranging trade. The opening two chapters of Amos describe the war crimes perpetuated by the surrounding peoples: torture, the killing of pregnant women, the capture and sale of war captives, unrestrained violence, and the desecration of the dead.

This perusal of Isaiah, Amos, and Micah demonstrates how hubris and its cruelties pervade civil, economic, and political life, whether among a people who claims to follow Yahweh or among those who make no such claim. The prophetic perspective on pride is expressed through noteworthy pictures of haughty men and women, of an official tossed far away like a ball, of kings cut down like a tree or covered in worms. The vocabulary of what hubris unleashes from positions of privilege and power against its victims also is stunning in its intensity: the vulnerable are crushed, trampled, destroyed, tortured, and

> And I will single out the world for its evil,
>   against the wicked for their crime,
> and put an end to the pride of the arrogant,
>   bring low the overweening of tyrants.
>
> Isaiah 13:11

sold. Violence abounded within Israel's and Judah's borders, but it also cut across the region in the atrocities of war.

The Judgment of God

While it is not uncommon to champion the moral sensibilities of the prophetic literature and its condemnation of injustice, in today's climate there can be a reluctance to accept the judgments that the prophets announced as God's response. This reticence to embrace that part of the prophetic message often is related to questions about divine violence.[26] The violence of God is a complex subject that I in no way minimize. Yahweh's judgment, however, is a crucial component of the prophetic imagination and is inseparable from its censure, so this unease requires comment. My purpose is to offer not an extensive apologetic but rather an introductory explanation of the significance of divine judgment for the prophetic imagination.[27]

The Old Testament is quite clear that since the creation Yahweh has been involved with humanity in *history*. God intervenes in the history of his people and of all the peoples of the earth to bless *and* to judge. What is it that leads God to judge?

26. An example of a critique of divine violence in the prophetic literature is Julia M. O'Brien, *Challenging Prophetic Metaphor: Theology and Ideology in the Prophets* (Louisville: Westminster John Knox, 2008).

27. The complexity of the issue means that no treatment will satisfy everyone. Recent popular treatments include Tremper Longman III, *Confronting Old Testament Controversies: Pressing Questions about Evolution, Sexuality, History, and Violence* (Grand Rapids: Baker Books, 2019), 123–206; Brent A. Strawn, *Lies My Preacher Told Me: An Honest Look at the Old Testament* (Louisville: Westminster John Knox, 2021), 31–53. For more technical discussions, see, e.g., M. Daniel Carroll R. and J. Blair Wilgus, "Introduction: What Do We Do with the God of the Old Testament?," and M. Daniel Carroll R., "'I Will Send Fire': Reflections on the Violence of God in Amos," in *Wrestling with the Violence of God: Soundings in the Old Testament*, ed. M. Daniel Carroll R. and J. Blair Wilgus, BBRSup 10 (Winona Lake, IN: Eisenbrauns, 2015), 1–14 and 113–32, respectively; and Carroll R., *Book of Amos*, 94–98; cf. J. Daniel Hawk, *The Violence of the Biblical God: Canonical Narrative and Christian Faith* (Grand Rapids: Eerdmans, 2019); Hemchand Gossai, *The Hebrew Prophets after the Shoah* (Eugene, OR: Pickwick, 2014).

Simply put, the judgment of Yahweh is the divine response to the persistent, toxic arrogance discussed in the preceding section. Hubris breeds injustice, which often leads to violence—whether socioeconomic, political, racial, or gendered violence (among others)—within and between nations. God cares about the poor and other vulnerable people.[28] History leaves no doubt that human evil knows no bounds, and the cost of its violence (financial, ecological, human, and more) is frightening. Jewish philosopher and public theologian Abraham Heschel aptly states, "That justice is a good thing, a fine goal, even a supreme ideal, is commonly accepted. What is lacking is a sense of the monstrosity of injustice."[29] Injustice in its various forms has characterized every society around the world from the beginning.

The demand for justice would be hollow without the assurance of accountability and confidence of concrete consequences for personal, familial, societal, national, and international injustice. Said another way, justice is impossible without judgment.[30] Every society recognizes this and stipulates penalties for all sorts of violations. In other words, they decree judgments for wrongs committed. Of course, societies make

28. Latin American liberation theology and Roman Catholic social doctrine stress what they call God's "preferential option for the poor," although its meaning and implications are contested. See Rohan M. Curnow, "Which Preferential Option for the Poor? A History of the Doctrine's Bifurcation," *Modern Theology* 31, no. 1 (2015): 27–59. Curnow's work does not include the pronouncements of Pope Francis, for which see, e.g., Francis, *Evangelii gaudium: Apostolic Exhortation on the Proclamation of the Gospel in Today's World* (Dublin: Veritas, 2013), §§186–216. I would state this biblical theme as God's "preferential option for the vulnerable" to reflect the breadth of divine concern.

29. Abraham Heschel, *The Prophets*, Perennial Classics (New York: Harper & Row, 2001), 260. Heschel was involved in social matters of his day, such as the civil rights and anti-war movements. He was a friend of both Martin Luther King Jr. and Reinhold Niebuhr.

30. For much of what follows, in addition to the resources in n. 27, see Terence E. Fretheim, *The Suffering of God: An Old Testament Perspective*, OBT (Minneapolis: Fortress, 1984), 107–66; Fretheim, *God and World in the Old Testament: A Relational Theology of Creation* (Nashville: Abingdon, 2005), 157–71. Also note the insightful article by J. Gordon McConville, "The Judgment of God in the Old Testament," *ExAud* 20 (2004): 25–42.

imperfect laws and imperfectly enact them, and they often fail terribly to establish justice, protect citizens, or promote their well-being and flourishing. Debates rightly rage about appropriate laws, enforcement, and penalties, yet all societies recognize that without legal structures and some system of punishment, social life degenerates into violent chaos. Importantly, the victims of injustice and of war cry out and insist that wrongdoers be held responsible and punished.

The ongoing challenge (here and around the world) is to consider how to properly address cultural prejudices and abuse, dysfunctional and inequitable structures, complicit leadership, and the ruthlessness of combat. The prophets tackle all of this head-on, but they do not simply denounce social ills and military excess. They proclaim that the sovereign God judges sins and systems that have gone unchecked.

To begin with, the Old Testament teaches that a moral order is woven into the very nature of things. Actions, good and bad, organically can harvest corresponding responses. So there are times when human violence spawns counterviolence as it turns on evildoers. There are instances, too, when creation itself reels from the effects of human sin or even becomes an instrument of judgment in God's hand (e.g., Amos 1:2; 4:6–10; cf. Deut. 28:20–24, 38–42).[31] God also can use other nations as agents to punish wrongdoing. In the eighth century BCE, the foreign power that enacted God's judgment against Israel and Judah was Assyria.[32] In sum, Yahweh judges through various means. Importantly, all of these judgments occur in *history*, the messy arena in which humanity embodies its hubris and effects its violence. Divine retribution for wrongs committed in history

31. Although the divine connection is not as direct in the deed-consequence pattern of the natural order, God did establish the moral constitution of creation.

32. Isaiah also mentions Babylon, not as an invader but rather as a defeated foe (Isa. 13–14; 46–47). Cyrus of Persia is mentioned as facilitating the return to the land (44:28–45:7). The Assyrians are identified specifically as Judah's enemy, principally in chaps. 8–10, 14, 20, 30–39 (cf. Mic. 5).

must occur within those same complex realities. The prophets usually do not know exactly when judgment would come, although they believe it to be imminent. They speak of it as a future time, the day of Yahweh, but do not predict its date.

The prophetic literature communicates divine judgment through its imagery and literary genres. These include the lawsuit, with its call for witnesses and declaration of guilt (e.g., Amos 3:1–4:13; Isa. 1:2–3; Mic. 6:1–8); the woe (e.g., Amos 5:18; 6:1; Isa. 1:4; 5:5–23; 10:1; 28:1; 29:1; 30:1; Mic. 2:1); and the many instances of phrases like "thus says Yahweh" (e.g., Amos 1:3; 3:11; 7:17; Isa. 22:15; Mic. 2:3; 3:5) that underscore the certainty of judgment. On occasion these speech acts are coordinated with a striking metaphor. For example, in an opening verse of Amos, Yahweh roars like a lion, setting an ominous tone for the rest of the book (1:2; cf. 3:8, 12). God will bring down the arrogant (e.g., Isa. 2:11–17; 3:17; 5:15; Mic. 2:3) and humiliate the proud as they are paraded away in defeat (Amos 4:3; 6:7). Such is also the destiny of nations and their leaders who consider themselves superior, as was mentioned earlier in connection with the shame to be brought on Assyria and Babylon (Isa. 10; 13–14; Mic. 5:5–6 [MT 5:4–5]). The guilt of leaders is weighty, extending beyond their own sin. They are the ones who lead their people to ruin and their nations to judgment. The blood of so many is on their hands.

Judgment reveals something fundamental about God's person, but it is important to approach this issue appropriately and with nuance. Judgment occurs because Yahweh is a God of pathos, one emotionally engaged with his creatures.[33] Arrogance and the injustice it generates make Yahweh (and his prophets) angry precisely because Yahweh is a God of justice and will not remain on the sidelines. Heschel comments, "As

---

33. See esp. Heschel, *Prophets*, 285–98; cf. Matthew R. Schlimm, "Different Perspectives on Divine Pathos: An Examination of Hermeneutics in Biblical Theology," *Catholic Biblical Quarterly* 69 (2007): 673–94.

long as the anger of God is viewed in light of the psychology of passions rather than in the light of the theology of pathos, no understanding will be possible."[34] Yahweh is not a detached, impassible deity; he cares and intervenes to punish wrong. Some wince at the mention of divine anger, but Heschel again hits the right key: "Admittedly, anger is something that comes dangerously close to evil, yet it is wrong to identify it with evil. It may be evil by association, but not in essence, . . . reprehensible when associated with malice, morally necessary as resistance to malice."[35] And again: "[Our] sense of injustice is a poor analogy to God's sense of injustice. The exploitation of the poor is to us a misdemeanor; to God, it is a disaster. Our reaction is disapproval; God's reaction is something no language can convey. Is it a sign of cruelty that God's anger is aroused when the rights of the poor are violated, when widows and orphans are oppressed?"[36] To confess that Yahweh gets angry is not the same thing as saying that Yahweh is an angry God, an irrational, vindictive deity. On the contrary, Yahweh's anger is occasional and focused. It arises because God is moved by human sin, and it is directed at moral violations that specific persons, groups, structures, and nations perform against others.

But there is more to be said about the divine pathos in judgment. To begin with, God's anger is inseparable from his mercy (Exod. 34:6–7; Jer. 18:1–10; Joel 2:13; Jon. 4:2; Nah. 1:2–8), and our three prophets declare this in several ways. First, Yahweh is not swift to judge. In the book of Amos, the structure of the Oracles against the Nations ("for three trespasses . . . and for four") suggests that God has allowed transgression to go on for some time before being compelled to act (1:3, 6, 9, 11, 13; 2:1,

34. Heschel, *Prophets*, 362; cf. M. Daniel Carroll R., "A Passion for Justice and the Conflicted Self: Lessons from the Book of Micah," *Journal of Psychology and Christianity* 25, no. 2 (2006): 169–76.

35. Heschel, *Prophets*, 360. For his discussion of divine anger, see pp. 358–92; cf. DeYoung, *Glittering Vices*, 137–62.

36. Heschel, *Prophets*, 365.

4, 6). The series of five warnings in 4:6–11, which each conclude
with "but you did not turn back to me" (4:6, 8, 9, 10, 11); the offers of life (5:4, 6, 14); and the willingness twice not to proceed
with judgment because of the prophet's intercession (7:1–6)
also demonstrate God's patience and a willingness to turn away
from judgment. Indeed, it pains Yahweh to carry out judgment
(e.g., Isa. 16:9–11; Amos 5:1).[37] It is God's "strange" work (Isa.
28:21), and its announcement brings no joy to the prophet (Isa.
6:11). We are told, too, on several occasions that God's anger
is for a moment and not permanent (e.g., Isa. 26:20; 54:7–8;
57:16–19; Mic. 7:18–20). Imagery, such as Yahweh as a nursing
mother who loves her child (Isa. 49:15–16; 66:13), challenges the
idea of a constantly enraged deity, and the portrayal of Israel
and Zion as his children, his daughter, and his wife underscore
Yahweh's devotion to his people.[38] "Comfort, O comfort, My
people," the prophet cries, for the time of judgment has passed
(Isa. 40:1). The limited time frame of judgment is reinforced by
the oracles of salvation, which is the topic of chapter 4 below.
Judgment is not the final word of God.

The prophetic announcement of imminent judgment would
have served several purposes. The proclamation of impending
doom would have forced the people of God to make choices.
What we have before us is literature with intent. Yahweh's desire
was for Israel and Judah to acknowledge and refrain from the
evil of their ways, their systemic injustice, and their unacceptable politics.[39] Yahweh had a covenantal relationship with this
people and was dedicated to their restoration. Amos, Isaiah,

37. For the lament of Amos 5:1 as Yahweh's and not the prophet's, see Carroll R., *Book of Amos*, 294–95.
38. Brittany Kim looks at Isaiah's household relational metaphors in *"Lengthen Your Tent-Cords": The Metaphorical World of Israel's Household in the Book of Isaiah*, Siphrut 23 (University Park, PA: Eisenbrauns, 2018). These various metaphors and their interrelationship admittedly are complex.
39. For a discussion of how unconditional prophetic announcements of judgment can be a legitimate call to repent, see Carroll R., *Book of Amos*, 90–94.

"In a brief moment I forsook you
   but with great compassion will I gather you in.
In surge of fury I hid My face from you,
   but with everlasting kindness I have compassion
      for you,"
   said your redeemer, the LORD.

Isaiah 54:7–8

and Micah constantly refer to this fact, both to indict and to encourage the people. A case in point is the utilization of the exodus. Because of their election and experience of redemption in the past, Israel stood condemned (Amos 2:9–10; 3:1–2; cf. 9:7). Their identity as the people of God meant that they were beyond excuse. Their faithlessness was a scandal. At the same time, in Isaiah the return from exile is fashioned as a second exodus by which God's people will witness anew Yahweh's strong arm on their behalf (e.g., Isa. 40:3; 43:1–7, 16–21; 48:20–21; 52:9–12; Mic. 7:15–17).

Tragically, apparently most chose not to relent from doing wrong or to recognize how infirm their social construct actually was; they could not fathom that God would insert himself into their history and bring an end to the world as they knew it (Amos 9:10; Isa. 29:15; 30:10; cf. Amos 5:14). Another wrongheaded strategy was to avoid (Isa. 39:1–4) or silence the prophets who spoke truth (Amos 2:11–12; 7:10–17)—not only truth to power, for that is too limited an appreciation of the prophetic task, but truth to all of Israel and Judah. The entire body politic had forsaken Yahweh, the prophets decried, and was fatally diseased. All stood guilty before God and were deserving of punishment (e.g., Isa. 1:2–6).[40] It was more palatable for Israel and Judah and their elites to heed prophets who for a

40. Also see the discussion in chap. 3 below.

price proclaimed an assuring word that all would be well (Mic. 2:6–7, 11; 3:5); these speakers of falsehood would have their own reward (Isa. 3:2; 9:13–17; 28:7–13; Mic. 3:6–7). For this audience, the prophetic proclamations were a final warning.

Amos, Isaiah, and Micah exposed and unsettled the webs of hypocrisy and the contextual contradictions of Israel and Judah. Opposition was inevitable. Several of these incidents are recorded in the text, most famously Amaziah's attempt to ban Amos from his calling and force him to return to Tekoa in his homeland of Judah (Amos 7:10–17; cf. Isa. 39). Isaiah had to respond to the phony religious confession of Ahaz, Judah's king, that aimed to conceal his negotiations with the Assyrians to ward off the impending attack by Aram (Syria) and Israel (Isa. 7:3–25; cf. 2 Kings 16:5–9). Micah condemned the prophets of the status quo and declared that justice empowered him to speak out (3:5–8).

Some, however, may have taken the hard messages of the prophets and their predictions of disaster to heart and changed their ways. Others, the victims of injustice, may have been reassured by the promise of judgment. What they had suffered had been laid bare publicly. The prophets also announced that one day the proud practitioners of evil would be punished. This indictment vindicated these victims and would have been an assurance of Yahweh's ethical commitments. This very different vision of reality could have served to encourage them to persevere through the coming judgment and endure its hardships, even if that might mean deportation and, possibly, death. They could rest in the truth that this was Yahweh's path to make things right in the rough-and-tumble vicissitudes of their history. The prophetic message disclosed the ugly sins of Israel, Judah, and the nations and decreed their demise. These words were distasteful to some but would have been a lifeline for the repentant and downtrodden. Judgment was a hope to be welcomed.

The Sociopolitical Prophetic Indictment Today

This has been a far-ranging chapter. We have looked at how Amos, Isaiah, and Micah denounced injustice in Israel and Judah. Each prophetic book, in its own unique way, communicates its message through powerful imagery and vignettes of confrontation. Their condemnatory words underscore foundational theological truths that should stimulate reflection on possible prophetic tasks by the faithful today.

To begin with, these prophets shed light on what Heschel calls the "monstrosity of injustice." They reveal the depths and the breadth of human cruelty and point to the hubris endemic to humanity as a key factor in injustice. This arrogance breeds attitudes, actions, and systems that enable the domination of others, and violence in its different forms often is the tool employed to maintain that injustice. Amos, Isaiah, and Micah did not limit their critiques to a few individuals or to the elites, although they were primary targets; these sins also were culturally and concretely systemic. Injustice infused multiple dimensions of national life.

The first lesson to grasp, then, is that the prophetic imagination (and the entire Old Testament) has an expansive appreciation of sin, which can help us recognize how pervasive and cruel it is and that it is individual, social, cultural, structural, national, and international.[41] It permeates every sphere of life, every group, every structure, every person. It is not difficult for us to point to unsavory individuals or groups whom we might know or who appear in the news. The fact that few transgressors are named by the prophets but instead are identified by their

---

41. John Goldingay perceptively titles his discussion of sin as "The Nightmare," in *Old Testament Theology*, vol. 2, *Israel's Faith* (Downers Grove, IL: IVP Academic, 2006), 254–349; also note Mark Boda, *A Severe Mercy: Sin and Its Remedy in the Old Testament*, Siphrut 1 (Winona Lake, IN: Eisenbrauns, 2009); Joseph Lam, *Patterns of Sin in the Hebrew Bible: Metaphor, Culture, and the Making of a Religious Concept* (New York: Oxford University Press, 2016).

ongoing activities or speech allows us to make those analogies quite easily. Personally or through other means, like the media, we know of people who mistreat the vulnerable, corrupt the legal process, show disdain for those who are of little consequence to them, and lead countries to war. Although twenty-first-century societies are quite different from ancient Israel, these character types persist across time and space. The text readily comes to life.

More difficult, and potentially unnerving, is the awareness of the broader realities of systemic injustice and cultural and national sins sparked by reading these prophetic books. Again, our world is not that of Israel's prophets, but these many dimensions of sin are a reality in every age. Although the mechanisms are not the same, the wheels of injustice still grind down the vulnerable. Examples of structural sin in the United States include race relations, mass incarceration, educational inequities, housing restrictions, and irregularities in voting rights and law enforcement. To these could be added the arrogance and lifestyles of the political classes, the discrimination endured by women, the tragic treatment of Native Americans, the checkered history of immigration and immigration law, intolerance toward Latino/a and Asian and Asian American communities, as well as the horrors of human trafficking, the opioid epidemic, and more. Each form of injustice has its own particular history and victims and spreads its tentacles into every corner of life, making everyone at some level a complicit participant.[42] The prophetic lens into human sin allows us to see the evils around us and to acknowledge that we inhabit a

---

42. Social science and historical research are necessary for realistic prophetic critique. This means becoming aware of the relevant data and interacting with hypotheses that attempt to explain them. These explanations can be contested by competing accounts. For example, witness recent arguments surrounding critical race theory or in the past over dependency theory, globalization models, components of certain Marxist thought (which actually is quite varied), and the military industrial complex idea, among others. The Spanish term *concientización* (the verb is *concientizar*) is pertinent here. It is the idea of raising awareness of these social realities through the Bible and social sciences, here as part of the prophetic task.

perverse social construction of reality. In so doing, we see the world truly. Whatever one's position on any of these issues, a prophetic vision recognizes the full reality of human evil and its cancerous presence. This more accurate perception is not a neutral exercise, which leads me to my second point.

The prophetic imagination is a disturbed one, one upset at injustice. But this is a theologically informed anger. In Amos, Isaiah, and Micah, prophetic invective is rooted in an extensive knowledge of the person and actions of Yahweh. Fundamentally, their rebukes are connected to the pathos of Yahweh. That is where legitimate prophetic emotion finds its source. Grounded in a divine call and bathed in scriptural traditions, the prophetic message was God's. This raises issues that those who claim the prophetic voice today must face honestly: What ultimately drives our prophetic passion? Is it the biblical text and a deep theology, or is it drawn more from a particular political ideology with its set of partisan commitments that determine what can and cannot be talked about and how? To what degree might it reflect the often acerbic and deliberately polarizing outlets of social media? Are the targets of our prophetic accusations determined primarily by a political party and its platform? Is our fund of texts limited to a few frequently quoted passages that can become slogans (e.g., Amos 5:24; Isa. 61:1; Mic. 6:8), or does our biblical foundation extend more broadly? To speak prophetically well is to be versed in the biblical text that gave birth to this voice.

Third, the prophetic imagination is committed and constant. In addition to the insights that it provides, a prophetic vision can motivate us to speak and act against wrong and the hubris that drives it. The prophetic stands in solidarity *with* and *for* the vulnerable and *against* perpetrators of injustice and sinful systems.[43]

---

43. There are many expressions of this stance. E.g., the first of the three Rs of the commitment of the CCDA (Christian Community Development Association) is "relocation." Michelle Ferrigno Warren uses the term *proximity* (*The Power of*

But—and this is crucial—our prophetic texts do not tell us *how* to fulfill this task in the twenty-first century. In these books we are given snapshots of what ancient prophets experienced in their contexts, not directives. In other words, we are left with a general mandate to denounce wrong. The prophets provide important theological grounding and a moral compass, but not policy blueprints. It is up to us to process what the prophetic imagination and course of action might look like today. These prophetic books also demonstrate that such involvements provoke reactions of various kinds (confrontation, silencing, marginalization), even from religious leaders and institutions. In these texts we see debates over the demands of the faith, the meaning of theological traditions, and the authority to speak. This always is the experience of the prophetic voice. With prophetic commitment will come clash.

A fourth lesson relates to the inclusion of judgment in the prophetic vision. This judgment may come via the organic processes of the moral constitution of creation or through other forces. Unlike the ancient prophets, however, we are not privy to the council of Yahweh (Amos 3:7). We cannot foretell the means or timing of divine judgment—even the biblical prophets did not predict dates—but we do know that one day it will come. It must, or prophetic denunciation loses credibility and is reduced to loud protest. Because they think God cannot see (even if they believe that he exists), the guilty must be told that they cannot trust their plans. Their sin matters to God, and there is a price to pay for injustice. At the same time, the victims of injustice need to hear that Yahweh has seen their suffering and heard their cries; they need to trust that one day God will act on their

---

Proximity: Moving beyond Awareness to Action [Downers Grove, IL: InterVarsity, 2017]). Liberation theology and others speak of "conversion" to the poor. Properly understood, this means the commitment to come alongside the vulnerable as the starting point for theology and mission. This is not a neutral position from afar, one without empathy or involvement.

behalf and punish evildoers.[44] Sinful cultures must realize that God will hold longstanding sinful attitudes, words, actions, and systems to account; nothing and no one are beyond God's reach. Ours must be a diatribe against evil *and* a declaration of divine intention.

Fifth and last, a full prophetic perspective requires more than critique. To denounce and deconstruct is one thing; to seek the repentance of the transgressors and the culture at large, or at least some admission of wrong that might recalibrate their perception of the world, is another (and perhaps costlier) challenge. For instance, even though he knew that Israel was guilty of sins at many levels and was deserving of punishment, Amos interceded with Yahweh to be merciful in judgment (7:1–6).

This aspect of the prophetic call always has been a quandary for those seeking change. How much time and effort does one dedicate to this often frustrating and fatiguing process in personal relationships, the workplace, education, and the public square?[45] Martin Luther King Jr. constantly dealt with this facet of his prophetic ministry, as have many others, but dealing with passivity or opposition is part of incarnating the prophetic vision. The biblical prophets do eventually reach a point when they cease such gestures and pronounce definitive and inescapable judgment—but Yahweh never gives up on his people or the nations, even when decreeing judgment. The warnings and the judgment were designed in part to have transgressors, indeed entire nations, bend the knee, and there always was a message of a hope beyond the time of divine visitation. How to

44. See, e.g., the reflections of the potential impact of the book of Nahum on the victims of the horrific violence of the Congolese war. Jacob Onyumbe Wenyi, *Piles of Slain, Heaps of Corpses: Reading Prophetic Poetry and Violence in African Context* (Eugene, OR: Cascade Books, 2021).

45. For instance, this is where recent discussions of the debated phrase *white fragility* come into play. Minorities can get exasperated at conversations and the pace of progress in racial- and ethnic-related matters. This kind of frustration extends, of course, to other social-ethical topics.

adjudicate this dimension of the prophetic must be determined on a case-by-case basis.

The discussion of the prophetic imagination, in one form or another, necessarily comes back to the person of Yahweh: who God is, what God demands, and what God will do. This fact explains the importance of the prophetic critique of religion, which is inseparable from the censure of social sins. The prophets understood that to denounce Israel and Judah's worship was to get at the heart of the matter. This is the topic of the next chapter.

3

"Let Justice Roll Down"
Worship and Social Responsibility

The Recurring Challenge

The storming of the Capitol Building in Washington, DC, on January 6, 2021, shook the nation. There are many topics to analyze about that singular event, but for this chapter my interest lies with one particular aspect. One of the ideologies motivating some of those who participated that day was a form of Christian nationalism. Such ideas have been brewing for some time, but they were ignited in significant ways by President Donald J. Trump.[1]

While some may be surprised at the religiously sanctioned nationalism or national exceptionalism that was on display that day, the wedding of faith, culture, and politics is as old as time. As we will see later, it was part and parcel of the religious world

1. Note, e.g., John Fea, *Believe Me: The Evangelical Road to Trump* (Grand Rapids: Eerdmans, 2018).

53

of the ancient Near East and a special target of the biblical prophets. Multiple examples of this coupling of religion and ideology can be drawn from Christian history. I present several to demonstrate that this has been a persistent challenge for the church. The prophetic critique is perennially timely.

I begin with sixteenth-century Spain. After centuries of conflict, the surrender of Granada in 1492 completed the *reconquista*[2] and marked the end of Moorish rule on the Iberian peninsula. The Spanish monarchy, strengthened by the marriage of Isabel I of Castilla and Fernando II of Aragón, subsequently launched the Inquisition. This context shaped the Spanish Catholicism that came to the Americas as a militant one, designed to conquer new lands for the crown and Rome.[3] Soon the violent expansion of the Spanish Empire prompted fierce debates about its right before God to forcefully subdue the Indigenous civilizations and the proper means of evangelization.[4]

The most famous theological confrontation, full of important juridical and political implications, occurred in 1550–51. The jurist Juan Ginés de Sepúlveda made the case for justifying Spain's subjugation of the native populations against the arguments brought by the Dominican friar Bartolomé de las Casas, who became known as the Defender of the Indians. To yoke the conquest with Catholic evangelization, Sepúlveda appealed to natural law, the superiority of Spanish civilization,

2. This is the Spanish term for the retaking of Spain from the Moors.

3. Luis N. Rivera, *A Violent Evangelization: The Political and Religious Conquest of the Americas* (Louisville: Westminster John Knox, 1992); Fernando Mires, *La colonización de las almas: Misión y conquista de Hispanoamérica*, Colección Universitaria (San José, Costa Rica: Editorial DEI, 1987).

4. These debates concerned, e.g., the use of force, the role of the *requerimiento* (a document in Spanish read to the Indigenous informing them of Spain's right to conquer them if they did not submit to the pope and the Spanish crown), the establishment of *encomiendas* and *reducciones* (the granting of land and the Indigenous of that land as labor to certain individuals; ideally this system was to provide the opportunity for evangelization of the unconverted), and the competing visions of the Franciscan and Dominican orders. For details see the sources in n. 3.

and biblical texts condemning idolatry.[5] Las Casas countered by condemning the horrors of those wars and the decimation of the Indigenous population through disease and forced labor.[6] He then proposed what he felt was a more Christlike way to persuade them to believe in Jesus and accept the Catholic religion.[7] Las Casas's decades-long efforts did have some positive impact with the proclamation of Paul III's papal bull *Sublimis Deus* (1537); the passing of the New Laws that, among other things, abolished the slavery of the Indigenous (1542–43); and his Verapaz ("True Peace") socioreligious experiment in what is today northern Guatemala. Yet Las Casas faced constant political intrigue and disappointments in the Americas and at the Spanish court.

A second example comes from Germany in the 1930s and 1940s. The political and economic turmoil after the First World War combined with other factors, such as historic German antisemitism and exceptionalist belief in the German *Volk*, drew the enthusiasm of many Protestants to the racialized ideology of Hitler's National Socialist Party. The result was the Reich Church (*Reichskirche*) of the German Christians (*Deutsche Christen*), who supported the Nazi regime and its aspirations. Their combination of faith and ideology, among other things, marginalized the Old Testament as a Jewish book, portrayed Jesus as an Aryan and not a Jew, and glorified the early military successes of the German war machine.[8] The Confessing Church

5. Juan Ginés de Sepúlveda, *Tratado sobre las justas causas de la guerra contra los indios* (Mexico: Fondo de Cultura Económica, 1941).

6. For the Indigenous perspective of the war and its consequences, see Miguel León-Portilla, ed., *Visión de los vencidos: Relaciones indígenas de la conquista*, rev. ed. (Mexico: Universidad Nacional Autónoma de México, 1992).

7. Bartolomé de las Casas, *The Only Way*, ed. Helen Rand Parish, trans. Francis Patrick Sullivan, Sources of American Spirituality (New York: Paulist, 1992); Gustavo Gutiérrez, *Dios o el oro en las Indias, siglo XVI* (Lima: Instituto Bartolomé de las Casas; CEP, 1989); cf. references in n. 3.

8. Doris L. Berger, *The Twisted Cross: The German Christian Movement in the Third Reich* (Chapel Hill: University of North Carolina Press, 1996); Richard Steigmann-Gall, *The Holy Reich: Nazi Conceptions of Christianity, 1919–1945*

(*Bekennende Kirche*) was born in reaction to these develop-
ments and sought to resist the subordination of the church
and its message to the totalitarian Nazi ideology. At a synod
convened in 1934, under the guidance of theologian Karl Barth,
a group of these pastors produced the Barmen Declaration,
which declares that Jesus Christ is the Lord of all life and that it
is to him, and not the state or its ideology, that the church owes
allegiance.[9] Many of the Confessing Church suffered for their
convictions. Some were imprisoned and exiled; others were
executed, most famously Dietrich Bonhoeffer, who struggled
mightily with what it meant to be a Christian and the church
in a "world come of age."[10]

The second half of the twentieth century saw the development of Latin American liberation theology, primarily within
Roman Catholic circles.[11] One of its central tenets was the need
to reform that church's structure and mission within a context
of massive poverty, sociopolitical and economic corruption,
and military dictatorships.[12] Liberation theologians accused the

(Cambridge: Cambridge University Press, 2003); Susannah Heschel, *The Aryan Jesus:
Christian Theologians and the Bible in Nazi Germany* (Princeton: Princeton Uni-
versity Press, 2008). There is ongoing debate concerning the stance of the German
Roman Catholic hierarchy and the Vatican toward the Nazi regime.

9. Fred Dallmayr, ed., *The Legacy of the Barmen Declaration: Politics and the
Kingdom*, Faith and Politics (Lanham, MD: Lexington Books, 2019).

10. This is Bonhoeffer's phrase to describe the condition of a world that no longer sees value in the church or God. See his *Letters and Papers from Prison*, trans.
Isabel Best et al., Dietrich Bonhoeffer Works 8 (Minneapolis: Fortress, 2010), and the
relevant sections of his *Ethics*, trans. Ilse Tödt et al., Dietrich Bonhoeffer Works 6
(Minneapolis: Fortress, 2005). Bonhoeffer was accused of being part of an assassination plot against Hitler. See Sabine Dramm, *Dietrich Bonhoeffer and the Resistance*,
trans. Margaret Kohl (Minneapolis: Fortress, 2009).

11. For its history and convictions, see Ignacio Ellacuría and Jon Sobrino, eds.,
Mysterium liberationis: Conceptos fundamentales de la Teología de la Liberación,
2 vols., Collección Teología Latinoamericana 16 (San Salvador, El Salvador: UCA
Editores, 1991); cf. David Tombs, *Latin American Liberation Theology*, Religion in
the Americas 1 (Boston: Brill, 2002).

12. Álvaro Quiroz Magaña, "Eclesiología en la Teología de la Liberación," in
Ellacuría and Sobrino, *Mysterium liberationis*, 1:253–72; all of section 2, "Iglesia
de los pobres, sacramento de la liberación," in Ellacuría and Sobrino, *Mysterium
liberationis*, 2:125–445; Edgardo Colón-Emeric, *Óscar Romero's Theological Vision:*

church hierarchy of not grasping the scale of these problems and worse, in some cases, of being complicit with reigning elites and the status quo. They proposed new models of being the people of God (such as the ecclesial base communities), developed new liturgies, and reconsidered the sociopolitical responsibilities of the church and the clergy.

The institutional church did respond constructively at some level, although there were tensions behind the scenes. After the landmark meeting of the Conference of Latin American Bishops (CELAM) at Medellín in 1968, which some believe launched liberation theology, the CELAM gatherings in Puebla (1979) and Santo Domingo (1992) grappled with articulating the identity and life of the Catholic Church in Latin America.[13] Debates continued, however, over the orthodoxy of liberation theology, especially its use of Marxism as an analytic tool.[14] But it was the challenge to the hierarchical church structure that was not tolerated (especially from 1980–86) by Pope John Paul II, and as a consequence several theologians were reprimanded (e.g., Ernesto Cardenal in Nicaragua) and silenced (Brazilian theologian Leonardo Boff).[15] It is important to point out that during this same period a group of evangelicals also was wrestling with the needs of the Latin American continent in relation to Christian tradition and mission. Although they did not suffer like some Catholic leaders, they did face serious opposition from church leaders, organizations, and mission

---

Liberation and the Transfiguration of the Poor (Notre Dame, IN: University of Notre Dame, 2018), 169–217.

13. The Aparecida conference (2007) occurred after these tensions. Argentine cardinal Jorge Bergoglio was in charge of drafting its final document, which reflected liberation concerns. He was elected in 2013 as the first Latin American pope (Pope Francis).

14. See the Vatican's Congregación para la Doctrina de la Fe, *Instrucciones sobre la Teología de la Liberación* (Madrid: Biblioteca de Autores Cristianos, 1986), and the rejoinder by Juan Luis Segundo, *Theology and the Church: A Response to Cardinal Ratzinger and a Warning to the Whole Church*, trans. John W. Dierksmeier (Minneapolis: Winston, 1985). The *Instrucciones* were produced by Cardinal Joseph Ratzinger, later Pope Benedict XVI, successor to John Paul II.

15. For a good overview, see Tombs, *Latin American Liberation Theology*, 227–55.

boards. From this group would arise the Fraternidad Teológica Latinoamericana (FTL).[16]

These cases illustrate the frequent co-optation of the Christian faith by political ideologies across the centuries. Each instance has a complex history from which it arose and is due to multiple factors. These systemic compromises cut across social groups and strata and had sociopolitical and economic aspects. They were not limited to certain elites but were broadly embraced by the general population and were part of the warp and woof of cultural life. In each case, contrary prophetic voices appeared for theological, missiological, and ethical reasons (all of which were inseparable from the other concerns). Standing against those popular ideologies generated opposition. I do not idealize the times or the people involved; one does not expect perfection in the personalities and positions of even well-intentioned Christians.[17] What these cases exemplify, however, is a consistent thread of prophetic pushback against the ethical failures of the Christian church.[18]

I now shift my attention to the United States. Here, too, one can draw on a number of examples. For instance, because of my Latino background and longtime involvement in immigration

16. J. Daniel Salinas, *Taking Up the Mantle: Latin American Evangelical Theology in the 20th Century* (Carlisle, UK: Langham Global Library, 2017); David C. Kirkpatrick, *A Gospel for the Poor: Global Social Christianity and the Latin American Evangelical Left* (Philadelphia: University of Pennsylvania Press, 2019). Founders of the FTL include René C. Padilla, Samuel Escobar, Pedro Arana, Pedro Savage, and my former colleague in Guatemala, Emilio Antonio Núñez. I have been a member since 1983. For frustration from a "mainline" perspective with denominational obstacles to moving beyond traditional doctrinal formulations ("Right-Doctrine Protestantism") to embrace a prophetic stance, see Rubem Álves, *Protestantism and Repression: A Brazilian Case Study*, trans. John Drury (Maryknoll, NY: Orbis Books, 1985).

17. E.g., for a time Las Casas advocated the importation of Africans to ease the demographic collapse of the Indigenous, a stance he later regretted; the Barmen Declaration did not address the matter of the treatment of the Jews, even though their persecution already was underway.

18. This is the argument that John Dickson makes for all of church history in *Bullies and Saints: An Honest Look at the Good and Evil of Christian History* (Grand Rapids: Zondervan, 2021).

reform, I could discuss how nativism and Christian faith have coalesced historically in response to the arrival of immigrants, refugees, and asylum seekers arriving from countries south of the border.[19] Another significant and persistent representative of the blending of faith and ideology in this country's history, with multiple implications for sociopolitical and economic life, has to do with racism,[20] which some call America's "original sin."[21] The presence of racism since the colonial period is well documented, but here I highlight the years preceding the Civil War.

Mark Noll calls this a time of "theological crisis," as both supporters of slavery and abolitionists appealed to biblical texts and themes to support their cause.[22] The hermeneutics of the proslavery position were fairly straightforward. From this perspective, the existence of slavery in both Testaments and the lack of a clear biblical statement condemning it contradicted any mandate to eliminate the institution. The abolitionist position was more indirect, appealing to transcendent principles, such as the value of all humans, and was harder to communicate than the apparently more commonsense readings of the Bible from the proslavery side. It was easier to secure agreement

19. The Catholic Church has a history of ministry to immigrants to the United States. See, e.g., essays in Daniel G. Groody and Gioacchino Campese, eds., *A Promised Land, A Perilous Journey: Theological Perspectives on Migration* (Notre Dame, IN: University of Notre Dame Press, 2008). For an account of evangelical involvements, see Ulrike Elisabeth Stockhausen, *The Strangers in Our Midst: American Evangelicals and Immigration from the Cold War to the Twenty-First Century* (New York: Oxford University Press, 2021). My latest book on immigration is *The Bible and Borders: Hearing God's Word on Immigration* (Grand Rapids: Brazos, 2020).

20. Mark A. Noll, *God and Race in American Politics: A Short History* (Princeton, Princeton University Press, 2010); Jemar Tisby, *The Color of Compromise: The Truth about the American Church's Complicity in Racism* (Grand Rapids: Zondervan, 2019); cf. Michael O. Emerson and Christian Smith, *Divided By Faith: Evangelical Religion and the Problem of Race in America* (New York: Oxford University Press, 2000).

21. Jim Wallis, *America's Original Sin: Racism, White Privilege, and the Bridge to a New America* (Grand Rapids: Brazos, 2016). Of course, racism has not been limited to African Americans. E.g., the peoples of Latin American and Asian descent have their own histories of racist experiences in the United States.

22. Mark A. Noll, *The Civil War as a Theological Crisis* (Chapel Hill: University of North Carolina Press, 2006); cf. Stephen R. Haynes, *Noah's Curse: The Biblical Justification of American Slavery* (Oxford: Oxford University Press, 2002).

that the treatment of slaves was abusive, but some interpreted
this as warranting only the reformation of the system, not its
demise. Arguments, pro and con, were designed either to buttress or to dismantle slavery and thereby impact the future
shape of the Union.[23]

The other religious world struggling with convictions of
faith at that time was that of the Black slaves themselves, the
very people whose lives and fates were being debated by white
constituencies. They, too, engaged the Bible but turned to different texts, particularly the exodus, and created alternative
forms of worship and church life that responded to the con-
straints of their circumstances.[24] Their biblical and theological
reflections responded to those systemic realities by confessing
faith in God's goodness and ultimate sovereignty to change
their existence, whether in this life or the next. These were not
theological ruminations of the comfortable or the privileged
but convictions born in the cauldrons of oppression. One of
the great legacies of slave religion to the Christian faith are
the Negro (or African American) Spirituals.[25] They eloquently
express the embodied pain and sorrow of the slaves while also
affirming life and hope in ultimate rest and vindication. Theirs
was a different Christianity with a different God than that of
the despotic context in which they labored. In his powerful
condemnation of the faith of slave owners, former slave,

23. Biblical arguments regarding race have continued since the Civil War, for
example, to defend segregation in some form. See, e.g., J. Russell Hawkins, *The Bible
Told Them So: How Southern Evangelicals Fought to Preserve White Supremacy*
(New York: Oxford University Press, 2021).

24. Eddie S. Gaude Jr., *Exodus! Religion, Race, and Nation in Early Nineteenth-
Century Black America* (Chicago: University of Chicago Press, 2000); Allen Dwight
Callahan, *The Talking Book: African Americans and the Bible* (New Haven: Yale
University Press, 2006); Rhondda Robinson Thomas, *Claiming Exodus: A Cultural
History of Mid-Atlantic Identity, 1774–1903* (Waco: Baylor University Press, 2013).

25. James Cone, *The Spirituals and the Blues: An Interpretation* (New York: Sea-
bury, 1972); Cone, *The Cross and the Lynching Tree* (Maryknoll, NY: Orbis Books,
2011), 1–29; Dwight Callahan, *Talking Book*; cf. W. E. B. Du Bois, *The Souls of Black
Folk* (New York: Modern Library, 1996), 252–67.

intellectual, and abolitionist Frederick Douglass states this fact with singular eloquence:

> Between the Christianity of this land, and the Christianity of Christ, I recognize the widest possible difference—so wide, that to receive the one as good, pure, and holy, is of necessity to reject the other as bad, corrupt, and wicked. To be the friend of one, is of necessity to be the enemy of the other. I love the pure, peaceable, and impartial Christianity of Christ: I therefore hate the corrupt, slave-holding, women-whipping, cradle-plundering, partial, and hypocritical Christianity of this land. Indeed, I can see no reason, but the most deceitful one, for calling the religion of this land Christianity. I look upon it as the climax of misnomers, the boldest of all frauds, and the grossest of all libels.[26]

The stories of early- to mid-nineteenth-century Black believers and preachers are sobering and inspiring, as are the spirituals, the "sorrow songs" (Du Bois's phrase), that still resonate today. African American Christians, and their biblical and theological scholarship,[27] continue to wrestle with staid orthodoxies that can marginalize their perspectives on faith, as witnessed in recent friction within local churches, denominations, and Christian institutions of higher education on matters of race.

These combinations of the Christian faith with sociopolitical and economic ideologies of what we would label the Left and Right and the extensive cultural affirmation they receive consistently have brought negative consequences to each

26. Frederick Douglass, *Narrative of the Life of Frederick Douglass*, ed. Deborah E. McDowell, Oxford World's Classics (Oxford: Oxford University Press, 1999), 101.

27. This field is immense and diverse in perspective. For biblical studies, see, e.g., Randall C. Bailey, ed., *Yet with a Steady Beat: Contemporary U.S. Afrocentric Biblical Interpretation*, Semeia Studies 42 (Atlanta: Society of Biblical Literature, 2003); Cain Hope Felder, *Stony the Road We Trod: African American Biblical Interpretation*, 30th anniv. ed. (Minneapolis: Fortress, 2021); Esau McCaulley, *Reading While Black: African American Biblical Interpretation as an Exercise in Hope* (Downers Grove, IL: IVP Academic, 2020); Nyasha Junior, *An Introduction to Womanist Biblical Interpretation* (Louisville: Westminster John Knox, 2015).

context and to the reputation of the church. The next section explores what this coupling of religion, ideology, and culture looked like in ancient Israel and Judah and why the prophets denounced it. At the same time, we must not reduce the prophetic critique of religion to the censure of civil religion. The previous chapter demonstrated that other issues also triggered prophetic concern over religious practices. Behind all of this, as we will see, lurked a more fundamental problem.

The Prophetic Critique of Religion

How do the books of Amos, Isaiah, and Micah grapple with the disconnect between the religious rituals of the people of God and their social ethics and with the delusions of civil religion? The prophetic message—and this is crucial—is that, at bottom, the people's misconceived faith betrays a deeply mistaken view of God. For the people of God to worship and not pursue ethics in their personal and social lives while linking Yahweh to a national ideology reveals that the deity they look to is *not* Yahweh. That deity, even if they call him Yahweh, is neither the God of their history nor the God of the prophets.

To speak of erroneous views of Yahweh is to move into a discussion of idolatry of a particular sort. This idolatry is not the worship of another god but the worship of *another Yahweh*. Other deities had their own names and identities and were connected to a different set of stories, religious practices, and sanctuaries. Much more difficult to parse out were flawed conceptions of Yahweh that appealed to the same traditions, performed the same rituals, and inhabited the same sanctuaries that were the substance of prophetic faith. How were the people to discern between these competing voices?

The academic study of idolatry in Old Testament scholarship usually concentrates on whether and to what degree the theological worldview and deities of the region influenced the religion of ancient Israel.[28] This has led to hypothetical historical reconstructions of the rise of Israelite monotheism and its aniconism (the prohibition of physical representations of God). There also are debates concerning popular religion in ancient Israel and the differences from and intersections with more official expressions of faith in Yahweh.[29]

Another way of looking at misconceptions of Yahweh—and it is the one pursued here—is to link idolatry to broader discussions of the nature and role of religion in society. Several disciplines can be helpful. A good place to start is a famous definition of religion by Clifford Geertz and interpretive anthropology.[30] This perspective dovetails with the earlier discussions on the prophetic imagination. According to Geertz, religion is "(1) A system of symbols which acts to (2) establish powerful, pervasive, and long-lasting moods and motivations in men by (3) formulating conceptions of a general order of existence and (4) clothing these conceptions with such an aura of factuality that (5) the moods and motivations seem uniquely realistic."[31]

28. For the history of research on Israelite religion, see Richard S. Hess, *Israelite Religions: An Archaeological and Biblical Survey* (Grand Rapids: Baker Academic, 2007), 25–80; Theodore J. Lewis, *The Origin and Character of God: Ancient Israelite Religion through the Lens of Divinity* (New York: Oxford University Press, 2020), 1–72. For a recent synchronic study of idolatry, see Thomas A. Judge, *Other Gods and Idols: The Relationship between the Worship of Other Gods and the Worship of Idols within the Old Testament*, LHBOTS 674 (London: T&T Clark, 2019).

29. M. Daniel Carroll R., "Reexamining Popular Religion: Issues of Definition and Sources; Insights from Interpretive Anthropology," in *Rethinking Contexts, Rereading Texts: Contributions from the Social Sciences to Biblical Interpretation*, ed. M. Daniel Carroll R., JSOTSup 299 (Sheffield: Sheffield Academic, 2000), 146–67; M. Daniel Carroll R., *The Book of Amos*, NICOT (Grand Rapids: Eerdmans, 2020), 70–73. For the archaeological data, see n. 28.

30. For this theoretical framework, see M. Daniel Carroll R., "Can the Prophets Shed Light on Our Worship Wars? How Amos Evaluates Religious Ritual," *Stone-Campbell Journal* 8, no. 2 (2005): 215–27, and the sources cited there; Carroll R., *Book of Amos*, 74–78.

31. Clifford Geertz, *The Interpretation of Cultures* (New York: Basic Books, 1973), 90; cf. Geertz, "The Pinch of Destiny: Religion as Experience, Meaning, Identity, Power," in *Available Light: Anthropological Reflections on Philosophical Topics* (Princeton: Princeton University Press, 2000), 167–86.

Said another way, religion defines and supports a certain social construction of reality. This can be "powerful, pervasive, and long-lasting," to use Geertz's words, because it is believed that the deity (or deities) established and sanctions it. Obviously, this social world depends on a particular understanding of the nature and will of the gods.

Religion creates and shapes a community in particular ways, including its values, laws, behaviors, cultural mores, socio-political and economic relationships and hierarchies, and more. This construct is legitimized through the performance of the religion's rituals led by specific intermediaries in designated sanctuaries. The ongoing observance of these communal rites serves to internalize this worldview across the entire community. These rituals become constitutive of everyday life. As a result, this all-encompassing ideology and its social reality are seen as natural, as true and divinely ordained.[32] This does not mean that these religious underpinnings are homogeneous or that allegiance is monolithic. Beyond the official religious paradigm, there are diverse opinions and religious views and practices. Even so, this overarching scheme is widely accepted.

This approach to religion and its rituals provides a useful framework for approaching the prophetic message within the religious world that was the ancient Near East. A relevant example from that context is the institution of kingship.[33] In Mesopotamia, it was believed that the gods founded the capital city and established kingship in a very distant past. Accordingly, that city and a people's monarch had a special relationship

32. For ritual theory in Old Testament studies, see Gerald A. Klingbeil, *Bridging the Gap: Ritual and Ritual Texts in the Bible*, BBRSup 1 (Winona Lake, IN: Eisenbrauns, 2007); more recently, his "Ritual Theology in/and Biblical Theology," in *The Oxford Handbook of Ritual and Worship in the Hebrew Bible*, ed. Samuel E. Ballentine (New York: Oxford University Press, 2020), 489–504.

33. John H. Walton, *Ancient Near Eastern Thought and the Old Testament: Introducing the Conceptual World of the Bible*, 2nd ed. (Grand Rapids: Baker Academic, 2018), 73–96, 253–68; Walton, *Old Testament Theology for Christians: From Ancient Context to Enduring Belief* (Downers Grove, IL: IVP Academic, 2013), 143–57.

with the gods, who were their patrons and protectors. The city would have housed the temple of the chief god (and potentially other gods), which was the earthly counterpart to the celestial residence. This cosmology conceived of the temple as the center of the universe and the sacred space from which the deity ruled. The architecture of the temple and the details of its ornamentation and furniture would have reflected these beliefs.

The king's palace stood in proximity to the temple, symbolizing the symbiotic relationship between the regime and the heavens. The correct performance of the rituals, the celebration of designated feasts, and the maintenance of the temple precincts and its personnel were fundamental to pleasing the gods. Fulfilling these duties was necessary for securing national peace and stability, the monarchy's success, and the people's well-being.

Israel's and Judah's complex religious worldviews overlapped with that of their neighbors, although there were significant differences as well. Two are important for the purposes of this chapter. The first has to do with ethics.[34] In the thought world of the ancient Near East, matters of morality dealt primarily with proper behaviors for maintaining the established socio-religious order. Being ethical was not a matter of imitating the gods, whose character could leave much to be desired. Rather, the goal was not to anger them and suffer punishment. Moral responsibility, as we would understand it, was not intrinsic to that theology, nor would the ancients have connected it to the evaluation of worship practices. This is quite different from the conviction that justice and compassion were central to Yahweh's person and deeply connected to worship.

The second issue is the ideological wedding of religion to politics in ancient Israel. When the monarchy was put in place by Yahweh, it came with warnings (1 Sam. 8:10–22; 12:13–25) and restrictions that countered common ancient criteria of kingly

---

34. Walton, *Ancient Near Eastern Thought*, 115–27.

greatness (Deut. 17:14–20).[35] This is quite a different account of royal beginnings! This perspective on the monarchy would allow for prophetic critique and confrontation. The theological underpinning of the Davidic promises and the election of Zion as Yahweh's dwelling place did not give carte blanche to Israel's kings. Yahweh's commitment was firm but conditioned on faith and obedience (2 Sam. 7:13–17). Neither the monarchy nor Jerusalem were invulnerable, as history would demonstrate.[36]

After the division of the United Monarchy, Judah maintained that theological framework. This created an ideological challenge for Jeroboam when he and the ten tribes broke away to establish a monarchy in Israel (1 Kings 12:25–33). He had to institute an alternative religious basis for the new regime. Because Jeroboam feared that the people might return to worship in Jerusalem, the location of Yahweh's temple and the capital of the Davidic dynasty, he selected two historic sanctuaries, Dan at the northern boundary and Bethel at the southern, as substitute sites and there set up golden calves.[37] Other priests were appointed, as was a new feast day. Jeroboam also had to secure a theological rationale for his throne other than the Davidic promises. The people had complained to Rehoboam of their burdensome "yoke" (12:3, probably a reference to taxes and forced labor), so Jeroboam appealed to the exodus, the

35. Robin Routledge, *Old Testament Theology: A Thematic Approach* (Nottingham: Apollos, 2008), 225–37; cf. Walter Brueggemann, *A Theology of the Old Testament: Testimony, Dispute, Advocacy* (Minneapolis: Fortress, 1997), 606–14.

36. For Zion theology, see John T. Strong, "Zion, Theology of," *NIDOTTE* 4:1314–21; Lewis, *Origin and Character of God*, 467–69. Brueggemann consistently evaluates Zion and Davidic theology in a negative light (e.g., *The Prophetic Imagination*, 40th anniv. ed. [Minneapolis: Fortress, 2018], 21–38; *Theology of the Old Testament*, 600–606, 657–58), but the biblical text distinguishes between a proper and a co-opted royal theology. For Zion in Isaiah, see Andrew T. Abernethy, *Discovering Isaiah: Content, Interpretation, Reception*, Discovering Biblical Texts (Grand Rapids: Eerdmans, 2021), 75–99.

37. The significance of the golden calves in that cultural context is disputed (Lewis, *Origin and Character of God*, 198–200), but the textual condemnation of this action is clear. See Lissa Wray Beal, *1 & 2 Kings*, Apollos Old Testament Commentaries 9 (Downers Grove, IL: InterVarsity, 2014), 183–85.

account of liberation from Pharaoh's oppression.[38] This was an earlier tradition than the Davidic one and went back to the very birth of Israel, a powerful theological justification for the Northern Kingdom.

When we turn to our three prophets' critique of the religions of Israel and Judah, we find that it is consistently scathing. They denounce both nations for severing rituals from ethical concerns and for a compromised faith in Yahweh that sanctioned the status quo and nationalist ideals. Each prophet expresses this differently, but there is no doubt as to how God viewed these religious social constructs.

Perhaps sarcastically mimicking a summons to worship, Amos calls Israel to go to the sanctuaries of Bethel and Gilgal—to "trespass" and to "continue to trespass" (4:4a). In other words, their worship is sin! After listing several rituals (none of which deals with sin or purification) and mocking their public display of frequent tithing, the prophet reveals the essence of the issue: "For so you have loved [to do]" (4:5). Truth be told, their ritual activity was nothing more than self-indulgence that fulfilled a religious impulse. Theirs was a Yahweh of their own creation, a deity shaped according to their tastes; he was an idol.[39]

Amos continues in 4:6–11 (this section is connected syntactically in the Hebrew to vv. 4–5) by listing judgments Yahweh has brought. Five times he says, "but you did not come back to Me." Israel has suffered hunger, drought, agricultural debacle, and military defeat but has refused to repent. All the rituals listed in verses 4–5 are expressions of gratitude to God for blessings, but clearly there is no reason for a celebratory faith! There is

38. In many ways Solomon had become Pharaoh. See J. Daniel Hays, "Has the Narrator Come to Praise Solomon or to Bury Him? Narrative Subtlety in 1 Kings 1–11," *Journal for the Study of the Old Testament* 28, no. 2 (2003): 149–74.

39. It is not that the people became like an object in creation that they worshiped, which is how G. K. Beale conceives of idolatry (*We Become What We Worship: A Biblical Theology of Worship* [Downers Grove, IL: IVP Academic; Nottingham: Apollos, 2008]). Rather, Yahweh had become a reflection of their vision of life.

> Therefore, this will I do to you, Israel,
>   because this will I do to you,
>   prepare to meet your God, O Israel.
>
> Amos 4:12

nothing for which to give Yahweh thanks! He in fact has worked against the people to somehow shake them into repentance. Their worship is divorced from the harsh realities that they are experiencing, and their God has been domesticated in praise. The series of disasters culminates in verse 12 with the challenge to prepare to meet the real Yahweh, whose overwhelming power is described in verse 13 (with five participles). To believe that they have been meeting Yahweh at the sanctuaries is a delusion, even if it is satisfying. The text gives the impression that all of the people are participating, which would include those suffering exploitation (2:6–8; 5:10–13; 8:4–6). Everyone has bought into the lie, even society's victims.

Amos 5:1–17 is an extensive chiasm[40] whose center and climax is at 5:8d: "Yahweh is his name" (author's translation). That is, the person of Yahweh is the focus of the passage:

A lament for Israel, vv. 1–3

  B seek Yahweh and live, vv. 4–6

    C warning to Israel, v. 7

      D the power of Yahweh to create, v. 8a–c

        E Yahweh is his name, v. 8d

---

40. Chiasms were a common literary technique in the ancient Near East. A chiasm is an inverted pattern, with matching passages that climax at the center. For this passage, see M. Daniel Carroll R., "Seek Yahweh, Establish Justice: Probing Prophetic Ethics; An Orientation from Amos 5:1–17," in *The Bible and Social Justice: Old Testament and New Testament Foundations for the Church's Urgent Call*, ed. C. Long Westfall and B. Dyer, McMaster New Testament Studies (Eugene, OR: Wipf & Stock, 2016), 64–83; Carroll R., *Book of Amos*, 289–91.

D′ the power of Yahweh to destroy, v. 9
C′ warning to the powerful, vv. 10–13
B′ seek Yahweh and live, vv. 14–15
A′ lament for Israel, vv. 16–17

Amos 5:4–6 calls Israel to seek Yahweh. In the ancient mind, as is evident in 4:4–5, to seek the deity meant going to the sanctuaries. These verses exhort Israel not to do that. (We already know what the people would do when they got there!) Instead, the matching lines of the passage in the chiasm (5:14–15) redefine what it is to seek Yahweh. It is to pursue and love the good and to establish justice at the gate.

The censure of Israel's religious distortions continues in 5:18–27, which also can be understood as a chiasm:[41]

A Day of Yahweh: unfounded longing, vv. 18–20
  B despised cult: unacceptable rituals, vv. 21–23
    C divine demand for justice, v. 24
  B′ despised cult: unlike the past, v. 25
A′ future reality: exile, vv. 26–27

I draw attention to the litany of rejected rituals in verses 21–23. Yahweh's rebuff of all these features of Israel's worship is visceral: "I hate," "I spurn," "[I] smell no," "I will not accept," "nor will I look," "take away from me," and "nor will I listen." This section also is very literary: seven rituals are cited in these verses. The totality of their activities is repugnant to Yahweh. The issue is not that Israel is not performing enough rituals or that it is performing them poorly. The rituals are problematic for another reason. Significantly, the center of this chiasm comes at 5:24, "But let justice well up like water and righteousness like a steady stream." Literarily and theologically,

---

41. See Carroll R., *Book of Amos*, 330–32.

the demand for ongoing, abundant justice is the focus of this critique.

The clash between Amos and Israel's religious ideology is narrated in 7:10–17. In line with the ancient context, Amaziah, the high priest, knows that the prophet's disapproval of Israel's religious activity goes hand in hand with a disapproval of the national ideology. Thus Amaziah notifies the king and accuses Amos of conspiracy (vv. 10–11), interpreting his prophesying as sedition. The high priest assumes that Amos speaks for a fee, but the prophet answers that his call is from Yahweh; he is beholden to no one (vv. 14–15). Amaziah's statement at verse 13 is telling: Bethel "is the king's sanctuary and a royal house." The union of the religious apparatus with the crown could not be clearer. Neither is the judgment on Amaziah. The nation will suffer defeat and exile, but the prophet announces that this fate will be personalized in the case of the priest because of the responsibility of his role before Yahweh and the people (v. 17).

The prophet's rejection of Israel's ideology actually starts at the very beginning of the book.[42] Amos 1:2 says that Yahweh speaks from Zion and Jerusalem, not from Bethel or Samaria— that is, from Israel's chief sanctuary or its capital city. In other words, Israel's entire religious ideology is illegitimate and finds no support from Yahweh. He is not even in Israel! To hold on to a hope of a future victorious day of Yahweh, thinking that he would defeat Israel's enemies, is ludicrous. That day will bring the darkness of inescapable defeat (the woe cry of 5:18–20) and exile (5:27). Israel's monarchy cannot be sustained. Hope of a future beyond the judgment lies not with the Northern dynasty but with David's in the South. Amos describes David's dynasty as a "fallen shelter" (9:11), as the days of glory had passed with

---

42. For a discussion of the breadth of this critique in Amos, with an eye to modern relevance, see M. Daniel Carroll R., "Imagining the Unthinkable: Exposing the Idolatry of National Security in Amos," *ExAud* 24 (2008): 37–54.

> And Isaac's high places shall be desolate,
> and Israel's sanctuaries shall become ruins,
> and I will rise against the house of Jeroboam
> with a sword.
>
> Amos 7:9

the division of the United Monarchy.[43] He avoids saying "house of David," which might have suggested his support of the current monarchy in Judah (that would be sedition!). But Amos is not a naive nationalist berating the rival kingdom to the north. Judah, too, is sinful (2:4–5; 6:1), as Isaiah and Micah later attest. Amos's is a Davidic hope in line with longstanding divine promises.

Amos announces that Israel's religious social imaginary is at its end. Judgment would begin at the national sanctuary at Bethel, leaving its singers silenced and dead everywhere (8:1–3).[44] It is there that Israel's ideology of a false Yahweh finds its primary religious endorsement through its rituals and the high priest. Bethel will be shaken when Yahweh actually stands in its precincts (9:1), and the horns of its altar are cut down (3:14). Israel's high places also will be destroyed (7:9). The scene in 9:1 follows the enigmatic 8:14 (cf. 2:8; 5:26), which could refer to belief in syncretistic local manifestations of Yahweh. This, too, is condemned, further dooming the religious world of Israel.[45]

In sum, Amos's message involves more than the people of Israel worshiping Yahweh without ethical conviction, more than their faith being content with current socioeconomic arrangements or being redirected by the national ideology. That

43. The meaning of the "fallen shelter of David" is debated. For a survey of views and the interpretation taken here, see Carroll R., *Book of Amos*, 508–11.

44. The Hebrew term for the place is *hêkāl*, which can mean "palace" or "temple." For the choice for "temple," see Carroll R., *Book of Amos*, 439–41, and many English versions.

45. Carroll R., *Book of Amos*, 467–73.

would be an inadequate reading of Amos's words. It would not be enough for the people to reform behaviors or separate out politics from their theology for the religious activities to be acceptable. What is ultimately at stake is the very person of Yahweh.[46] Bifurcating Yahweh from morality and manipulating worship for political ends or ignoring social ills reveals that it is *not* Yahweh whom they worship. *Their* Yahweh has been tailored to fit their religious and ideological desires. The *true* Yahweh despises that farce and in sharp finality announces the demolition of the sanctuaries, those places where that false Yahweh has been legitimated in sacrifice and song.

Isaiah's perspective on worship is grounded in the call narrative of chapter 6. The prophet sees the overwhelming presence of the Lord, Yahweh of Hosts, exalted and seated on his throne in the Jerusalem temple and surrounded by angelic beings ready to do his bidding (vv. 1–4).[47] The prophet is stunned by the scene and confesses his unworthiness to appear before the Cosmic King (cf. 66:1) and be commissioned into divine service (6:5–7). Such is the Most Holy One who is to receive the worship of his people in that sacred space. Is this the God of Judah's worship? The answer comes in the first chapter of the book.

Isaiah's first diatribe against Judah's religion appears in Isaiah 1:10–20. It starts with a comparison of Judah to Sodom and Gomorrah, which is followed by God's piercing question, "Why need I all your sacrifices?" (v. 11a). Yahweh then lists every conceivable ritual (this is a very religious people!) only to unreservedly reject them all (vv. 11b–15). The first-person verbs ("I am sated," "I do not desire," "I cannot bear," "I utterly despise," "I avert My eyes," "I do not listen"), as in Amos

46. This point is made as well by variations of the statement "Yahweh is his name" (4:13; 5:8, 27; 9:6).
47. Some argue that this is the heavenly temple, but see H. G. M. Williamson, "Temple and Worship in Isaiah 6," in *Temple and Worship in Biblical Israel: Proceedings of the Oxford Old Testament Seminar*, ed. John Day (London: T&T Clark, 2007), 123–26.

> Wash, become pure,
> > Remove your evil acts from My eyes.
> > > Cease doing evil.
> Learn to do good,
> > seek justice.
> Make the oppressed happy,
> > defend the orphan,
> > > argue the widow's case.
>
> Isaiah 1:16–17

5:21–23, reveal the depth of the dismissal of these activities. The people's hands are full of blood (Isa. 1:15). In an ironic double entendre, the blood may refer to the blood of the sacrifices or, as these activities are connected to commands to care for the vulnerable (v. 17), to the blood of the oppressed (cf. 59:3). The people's sin is like scarlet, red like the blood on their hands. Pointedly, their worship is the sin of which they must repent or be judged (1:18–20). This passage is echoed later in 29:13–14, which again hits at empty, busy religiosity. Seemingly, Yahweh has become a burden, since they do not bring worthy offerings (43:23–24). The once faithful city of Jerusalem, the chosen city of Yahweh's temple and worship, has become a whore (1:21).

There are two other extensive passages on religious practices. The first, 56:1–8, begins the censure of the people's Sabbath keeping with the demand for justice (v. 1). Doing justice is fundamental to not profane the Sabbath (v. 2). Then, in a surprising move, Yahweh states that he will embrace and abundantly bless two marginalized groups in Israel, foreigners and eunuchs[48] who honor the Sabbath (vv. 3–4, 6). The passage is profuse in

---

48. Early on, the term *eunuch* (*sārîs*) referred to important officials in political or military roles (e.g., Gen. 37:36; 1 Sam. 8:15). Later the term was used for castrated males employed in foreign royal courts, e.g., to supervise the king's harem. In Isa. 56:3, the eunuch is a castrated male incapable of producing offspring ("I am a withered

> Is this not the fast that I choose—
>   to unlock the shackles of wickedness,
>   and loosen the bonds of the yoke,
> to set the downtrodden free—
>   and to break every yoke?
>
> Isaiah 58:6

its description of the righteousness of their devotion in contrast to the religiosity of the community that dishonors the Sabbath by, as a later passage reveals (58:13–14), pursuing their own desires (cf. Amos 4:5).[49] The foreigner shall be brought into joyful participation in the temple rituals and no longer be an outsider (Isa. 56:7); the eunuch will receive a name that will endure forever (v. 5).

The second passage, 58:1–12, immediately labels the people's fasting as sin (v. 1). As we see in Amos and in our other passages in Isaiah, the community was religiously active (v. 2).[50] Yet theirs was a communal obtuseness that expected a reward for religious observance and self-denial, an attitude that aligned with the ancient Near Eastern mindset (vv. 2b–3a). Their cruelty toward others and the arrogance of their piety, however, are an indictment of their fasting (vv. 3b–5). The fast that Yahweh accepts requires self-denial and investment of a different kind: that which alleviates oppression and offers concrete compassion toward the needy (vv. 6–7; cf. v. 10). It is not that these must

---

tree"), which meant that there would be no descendent to carry on his name. For the different nuances of the term, see Gordon H. Johnson, "srys," *NIDOTTE* 3:288–95.

49. Some English versions translate the Hebrew term *ḥēpeṣ* in 58:13 as "pleasure" (ESV, HCSB, NASB; cf. NIV), others as "affairs" (NRSV, Alter) or "business as usual" (CEB). These renderings are possible, but it also appears in 58:3, where "pleasure" might make more sense. The verbal form occurs in 58:2.

50. Alter gives the verbal forms in v. 2 a jussive sense ("Let them seek, let them desire"). Other English versions translate these as iterative imperfects ("They seek . . . and delight"), which is my preference.

accompany fasting; the text says that *this* is the fast that Yahweh chooses. Fulfilling that demand would yield the restorative blessings that the fasting has tried to secure (vv. 8–12). Said another way, private piety is inseparable from public responsibility.

In the book of Amos, the national ideology is reflected in the unfounded confidence that Israel has in its strength and in Yahweh's protection. This is not the case in Isaiah, where we find the opposite problem: Judah wonders how Yahweh, the God of such a small country, would stack up against the deities of empires.[51] In the previous chapter, we looked at how Yahweh decreed the humiliation of the Assyrian king (Isa. 10) and defeated its imperial army at the siege of Jerusalem (chaps. 36–37). The taunting of the Rabshakeh at the walls of Jerusalem carries unmistakable theological import when he says that Yahweh in his anger has allowed the defeat of the rest of the country and that Yahweh, like the other gods of other conquered peoples, is incapable of defending his people (36:15–20).[52] Yahweh responds to Hezekiah's supplications for help by announcing that Assyria will pay for this mockery (37:21–29, 33–35).

In Isaiah 40–66, when God's people apparently find themselves in exile in Babylon, the theological stakes were high. A defeated people means a defeated deity. How could Yahweh prove his unrivaled sovereignty and superiority over the gods of Babylon when, in the ancient mind, the political realities that they could see with their own eyes were clear evidence that this was not true! As Yahweh lays out the promises to bring the people back to the land, he must convince them of

51. Misguided certainty in Yahweh's unconditional defense of Jerusalem does occur later in the days of Jeremiah (e.g., Jer. 7:1–4). The miracle of the deliverance of the siege of 701 (Isa. 36–38) may have been a key factor in producing that ideology. For details, see the sources in nn. 33, 36.

52. For the theological ideology of the Assyrians, see Mario Liverani, *Assyria: The Imperial Mission*, Mesopotamian Civilizations 21 (Winona Lake, IN: Eisenbrauns, 2017), 1–40; cf. above chap. 2, n. 20.

his incomparability and capabilities. They must see that the other gods are nothing more than images shaped by human hands (40:18–20; 41:6–7; 44:9–20; 46:1–2, 7).[53] Crafted idols are no match for the Creator (e.g., 40:21–31; 45:12, 18), the only God (40:25; 45:5–6; 46:9). Only Yahweh knows the future and controls history (41:21–29; 43:8–13; 44:24–28; 45:20–21). To trust in other gods is the epitome of foolishness.[54] This sovereign Holy One, Yahweh, is the God of Isaiah 6, the God of justice and compassion. This is the vision of God that should drive worship.

The book of Micah begins with a jolt. Yahweh announces coming in judgment with impressive power, beginning with the high places (1:2–3). Yahweh will depart from the temple in Jerusalem, but then he says that Jerusalem is Judah's high place (1:5)! This is ominous indeed, as that temple will be a target of his wrath. Because of unscrupulous religious leaders who can be bribed (3:5–7, 11) and the veneration of other deities (5:12–14 [MT 5:11–13]), the capital city and Zion would become a heap of ruins (3:12).[55] Their perverted concept of Yahweh is evident in their worship, most memorably censured in 6:1–8.

---

53. The lexicon in Isa. 40–66 for idols and their worship centers is large. See Andrew Davies, *Double Standards in Isaiah: Re-evaluating Prophetic Ethics and Divine Justice*, BibInt 46 (Leiden: Brill, 2000), 94. José Luis Sicre argues that Isaiah condemns the idols of foreign powers and money in *Los dioses olvidados: Poder y riqueza en los profetas preexílicos*, Institución San Jerónimo para la Investigación Bíblica 3, Estudios de Antiguo Testamento 1 (Madrid: Cristiandad, 1979), 51–64, 117–23. He also sees the idol of goods and money in Amos and Micah (pp. 109–16 and 124–30, respectively).

54. See the helpful discussion of these and other matters in Christopher J. H. Wright, *The Mission of God: Unlocking the Bible's Grand Narrative* (Downers Grove, IL: IVP Academic, 2006), 136–88. This discussion is reproduced in his *"Here Are Your Gods": Faithful Discipleship in Idolatrous Times* (Downers Grove, IL: IVP Academic, 2020), 1–65; cf. Daniel I. Block, *For the Glory of God: Recovering a Biblical Theology of Worship* (Grand Rapids: Baker Academic, 2014), 29–35.

55. See R. W. L. Moberly's intertextual readings of Mic. 3 with Ps. 46 and Jer. 7 regarding the delusions of a misdirected Zion theology in his *The God of the Old Testament: Encountering the Divine in Christian Scripture* (Grand Rapids: Baker Academic, 2020), 203–37.

> Her chieftains judge with bribes,
>   and her priests instruct for payment,
> and her prophets divine for silver
>   and on the LORD they lean, saying,
> "Is not the LORD in our midst?
>   No harm will come upon us."
> Therefore, because of you,
>   Zion shall be plowed like a field,
> and Jerusalem become heaps of ruins
>   and the Temple mount a high forest.
>
> Micah 3:11–12

These are some of the most well-known verses in prophetic literature. Micah 6:8 is preached in sermons, posted on websites, used as the foundation for justice ministries, and celebrated in song. It reads,

> It was told to you, man, what is good
>   and what the LORD demands of you—
> only doing justice and loving kindness
>   and walking humbly with your God.

Many cite this verse in isolation, unaware that it is the culmination of what some label a covenant lawsuit that begins in 6:1. There Yahweh announces that he has a case to bring against the people and calls nature as a witness. God is upset with Judah. In the following lines the word "what" (*mâ/meh*) is repeated several times: *What* has Yahweh done to deserve Judah's rebellion? In the past, Yahweh has redeemed them and raised up leaders, whereas *what* others have done is seek to curse them (vv. 3, 5).

The people's reply comes in verses 6 and 7. Note the echo of the key word: "With *what* shall I come before the LORD?"

(v. 6a, emphasis added). Now come rhetorical questions listing potential sacrifices with increasing hyperbole. The answer to the questions often is assumed to be a categorical no. But this is incorrect! In the ancient mindset, the way to appease an angry god is to offer sacrifices, and Yahweh is unhappy with the people. Of course, the deity would be pleased if they brought gifts! The more the better! Had not Solomon offered an extravagant number of oxen and sheep at the dedication of the temple (1 Kings 8:63)? The mention of possibly offering the firstborn, however, would have brought them pause (Mic. 6:7b). That was a pagan rite (cf. Lev. 18:21; Deut. 12:32) and a direct violation of God's will. That most extravagant gift would never be acceptable.

Yahweh responds in verse 8. Again, listen for the key term that knits together 6:1–8: "It was told to you . . . *what* is good and *what* the LORD demands of you" (v. 8, emphasis added). They do not know *what* Yahweh desires from them, so here God tells them *what* he seeks. As with our other two prophets, the problem is that the people do not know the true person of Yahweh. Their perceptions are culturally determined. They believe that Yahweh is like the other gods and conceive of worship accordingly, in this case as placating the deity. Relating ethical demands to a god's character and moral expectations does not fit that paradigm. Israel is worshiping *another* Yahweh. The following verses (vv. 9–16) are proof of how far Israelite society had strayed from acceptability before God, violating what is stipulated in verse 8.

The words of sinful religious leaders suggest that they believe in the national ideology of the invulnerability of Zion: "Is not the LORD in our midst? No harm will come upon us" (Mic. 3:11). The next verse puts the lie to that misplaced confidence. Zion and Jerusalem are facing destruction (v. 12). Ironically, this prophet's name, Micah, means, "Who is like Ya" (an abbreviated form of Yahweh). That is the very question that Judah has to answer.

The Prophetic Vision and Worship Today

Worship has become a popular topic in recent years. In North America discussions have revolved around, for instance, styles of worship, and a variety within evangelical and mainline Protestant traditions vie to be both true to the tenets of the Christian faith and relevant to an ever-changing culture.[56] Progressive voices, calls for multiethnic churches, and the new monasticism, among others, are seeking to reformulate worship in ways that resonate with their commitments.[57] I do not minimize these important considerations. I would like to focus the conversation, however, in a particular direction.

At least two concerns requiring careful reflection arise from the critique of religion in Amos, Isaiah, and Micah. The first is the matter of idolatry, which we introduced earlier in this chapter. Recent works on idolatry that have church leaders and lay people as their target audience commonly identify as idols aspects of the culture that draw believers away from a more singular commitment to the God of Scripture, because these items respond to people's fears or aspirations.[58] Cultural realities that commonly are mentioned include consumerism and prosperity, entertainment and social media, nationalism, and self-actualization, all of which have their own appointed spaces, regular activities and rhythms, vocabularies and talking points, gurus, and rewards— and all have seeped into the life and worship of the church.[59]

---

56. Paul A. Basden, ed., *Exploring the Worship Spectrum: 6 Views*, Counterpoints (Grand Rapids: Zondervan, 2004).

57. Two excellent examples are Soong-Chan Rah, *Prophetic Lament: A Call for Justice in Troubled Times* (Downers Grove, IL: IVP Books, 2015); Sandra María Van Opstal, *The Next Worship: Glorifying God in a Diverse World* (Downers Grove, IL: IVP Books, 2015).

58. Stephen E. Fowl makes the helpful distinction between the idolatry of believers and that of unbelievers in *Idolatry* (Waco: Baylor University Press, 2019), 5–9. Like Fowl, our focus is on the idolatry of believers. Another helpful observation that Fowl makes is that the fall into idolatry is incremental, not an intentional decision.

59. E.g., see James K. A. Smith, *Desiring the Kingdom: Worship, Worldview, and Cultural Formation*, Cultural Liturgies 1 (Grand Rapids: Baker Academic, 2009),

These observations are correct up to a point, but they can miss the essential issue at stake in worship, which is the person of God.

Our three prophets battled erroneous understandings of Yahweh and belief in other deities that impacted the people's understanding of God. Israel and Judah were supremely active religious nations, but the quantity of rituals did not qualify the worship as acceptable. From the prophets' perspective, these activities were directed at another god constructed according to the worshipers' tastes and needs. Their religion, in all of its expressions, had been co-opted by cultural givens and national ideologies. The people crowded the sanctuaries for worship, but they were petitioning and praising the communal idol they called Yahweh, who they thought would preserve their societies, bless them with bountiful crops, and secure victory for their armies. Their religious world was a complex lie sustained by religious practices and institutions. This explains why these prophets attacked the religious leadership, those who were charged with leading the people to true faith, and announced the destruction of the central sanctuaries. Reorienting the people's view of Yahweh and thus their social construction of reality would require the end of religion as they knew it before there could be a fresh encounter with the true God. Yahweh would not be mocked.

However one evaluates Latin American liberation theology, these theologians grasped this essential issue as they wrestled with the classic theological formulations of their tradition in the effort to address injustice and despotic dictatorships. Appealing to the category of idolatry, Pablo Richard says, "The fundamental theological task in Latin America is not so much to prove the existence of God, but rather how to discern the

89–129; Fowl, *Idolatry*; Wright, *"Here Are Your Gods,"* 93–102; Mark Labberton, *The Dangerous Act of Worship: Living God's Call to Justice* (Downers Grove, IL: IVP Books, 2012), 61–77. This list pertains to the United States and may be different in other parts of the world.

true God from false idols. The problem is not to know *if* God exists, but to demonstrate in *what kind* of God we believe."[60] This is akin to the prophetic charge long ago in their ancient contexts, and it remains so today.

What we witness in debates over coordinating current justice issues with the meaning and viability of the label "evangelical,"[61] over the substance of curricula in theological and ministerial training, over denominational histories and their future direction, over sociopolitical alignments and involvements, and the like is, at bottom, a struggle over the identity of the God we worship and the relationship of that God to matters of justice and compassion. This is a messy, stormy time of friction and hyperbole, of soul-searching and vitriol, of personalities and agendas, of institutional inertia and reform. This is a necessary travail, another moment in the history of the Christian church in this country in which to wrestle with the questions about who Yahweh is and what he requires of us. The Spanish word *coyuntura* is apropos here. A coyuntura is a moment when things come together in an important way. The church faces a significant coyuntura today. These struggles in the case of the prophets were intertwined with an unwavering commitment to the people of God. They were his people despite everything. So today, in our coyuntura, the prophetic voice ideally remains committed in some way to the church.

---

60. "La tarea teológica fundamental en América Latina no es tanto probar la existencia de Dios, sino discernir al Dios verdadero de los ídolos falsos. El problema no es saber *si* Dios existe, sino demostrar en *cuál* Dios creemos." Pablo Richard, "Teología en la teología de la liberación," in Ellacuría and Sobrino, *Mysterium liberationis*, 1:207. For an early foray into this discussion, see Juan Luis Segundo, *Our Idea of God*, trans. John Drury, A Theology for Artisans of a New Humanity 3 (Maryknoll, NY: Orbis Books, 1974).

61. Note, e.g., Mark Labberton, ed., *Still Evangelical? Insiders Consider Political, Social, and Theological Meaning* (Downers Grove, IL: IVP Books, 2018); Dan Stringer, *Struggling with Evangelicalism: Why I Want to Leave and What It Takes to Stay* (Downers Grove, IL: InterVarsity, 2021). Tensions over social issues within evangelicalism are not new. See, e.g., David R. Swartz, *Moral Minority: The Evangelical Left in an Age of Conservatism* (Philadelphia: University of Pennsylvania Press, 2012).

These difficulties lead to the second issue for reflection, which is the role of liturgy in getting God right. There are a number of Old Testament scholars who are aware of the power of liturgy and its relationship to ethics and whose work is important.[62] Their work can be correlated with perspectives on liturgy developed by several theologians.[63]

To begin with, there is no such thing as a nonliturgical church. Even those who claim to eschew liturgy congregate at the same time and place, consistently structure the service in the same way each Sunday (or Saturday), celebrate Christian ordinances (such as baptism and the Lord's Table) in a regular manner, use a standardized religious vocabulary and music repertoire, and contract religious personnel. It is more correct to say that these churches do not follow one of the historical liturgies of the church, but they do have a liturgy. What follows, then, applies to all Christian churches.

Liturgies, whatever they may be, are deeply instructive and formative. Liturgies are instructive in that they project and inculcate a certain understanding of God and a vision of the world and of the life of the people of God in the world. They do this through their various components (prayer, singing, the spoken word, the Lord's Table, and other features, depending on the church tradition). These activities, in the language of virtue eth-

62. Note Walter Brueggemann, *Israel's Praise: Doxology against Idolatry and Ideology* (Philadelphia: Fortress, 1988), 1–28; Samuel E. Ballantine, *The Torah's Vision of Worship*, OBT (Minneapolis: Fortress, 1999); Gordon J. Wenham, *Psalms as Torah: Reading Biblical Songs Ethically*, STI (Grand Rapids: Baker Academic, 2012); cf. John Goldingay, *Old Testament Theology*, vol. 3, *Israel's Life* (Downers Grove, IL: IVP Academic, 2009), 16–29 passim.

63. E.g., from different frameworks, James K. A. Smith, *Desiring the Kingdom*; Smith, *Imagining the Kingdom: How Worship Works*, Cultural Liturgies 2 (Grand Rapids: Baker Academic, 2013), 151–81; Fowl, *Idolatry*; Stanley Hauerwas, "Suffering Beauty: The Liturgical Formation of Christ's Body," in *Performing Faith: Bonhoeffer and the Practice of Nonviolence* (Grand Rapids: Brazos, 2004), 151–65; Myles Werntz, *From Isolation to Community: A Renewed Vision for Christian Life Together* (Grand Rapids: Baker Academic, 2022); Luke Bretherton, *Christ and the Common Life: Political Theology and the Case for Democracy* (Grand Rapids: Eerdmans, 2019), 212–17.

ics, are practices that shape—consciously or unconsciously—the dispositions, habits, and character of the participants.[64] These formative and instructive dimensions are inseparable; they mutually reinforce and build off one another.

In Amos, Isaiah, and Micah worship is flawed—not because it was not done according to historic scripts or because of a lack of passion. Rather, the God of Israel's and Judah's worship was not Yahweh. Their religious practices were producing and legitimating societies of greed, corruption, socioeconomic casualties, and national arrogance that were unacceptable to Yahweh and deserving of judgment. The creation of a culturally and ideologically pleasing God had yielded a world that the prophets condemned.

There is much here that carries over to our day. In light of what we have seen in Amos, Isaiah, and Micah, the essential question for a worship service must not be, as it often is, Did you like it? The questions that need asking are, What is the God of this worship like? Does this worship shape the congregants to be and live commensurate with the God of the prophets? If justice and compassion are part of the essence of who that God is, then are the people of God more just and compassionate because they have worshiped? If not, why not? Discussion about worship now moves into considering how it might contribute to creating a people of virtue. Evaluation is based less on musical excellence, beautiful venues, technologies, growing numbers, or emotional appeal but instead on faithfulness to *this* God at home, in the workplace, and on the street—a faithfulness visible in the virtues of justice, peace, hospitality, and solidarity as a testimony of and testament to the living God. A people

64. For the application of virtue ethics to Amos and Micah, see M. Daniel Carroll R., "Seeking the Virtues among the Prophets: The Book of Amos as a Test Case," *ExAud* 17 (2001): 77–96; Carroll R., "'He Has Told You What Is Good': Moral Formation in Micah," in *Character Ethics and the Old Testament: Scripture and Moral Life*, ed. M. Daniel Carroll R. and Jacqueline Lapsley (Louisville: Westminster John Knox, 2007), 103–18.

thus formed and grounded are less likely to be compromised by cultural trends and the political persuasions of the Left or the Right.[65] They will be more sensitive to the influences that corrupt the biblical vision of God. They will have a substantive counternarrative to unmask captivating cultural stories. Worship becomes inherently deeply confessional and missional.

For marginalized groups, worship can be a haven, a time and place to heal congregants of the many difficulties of living as a minority or to provide social services or to organize for community and political projects to respond to concrete needs. Yet these churches cannot be idealized. They, too, can be influenced negatively by cultural and ideological trends and so compromise the faith.[66]

I am not advocating a particular worship style. Instead, the plea is to align worship with the prophetic imagination, which demands that it present the biblical God and be a means of creating a community of faith as it was designed to be. Stanley Hauerwas is correct when he observes the serious consequence of bifurcating liturgy from ethical responsibility: "When liturgy becomes a motivation for action that does not require the liturgy for the intelligibility of the description of what we have done, then we lose the means as Christians to make our lives our own."[67] Liturgy should not just encourage us to act justly

---

65. Although James Davidson Hunter's *To Change the World: The Irony, Tragedy, and Possibility of Christianity in the Late Modern World* (New York: Oxford University Press, 2010) has been criticized on several levels, the warnings about the co-optation of Christians across the political spectrum are worth considering. Note the careful summaries and evaluations of the political philosophies of various Christian traditions in Bretherton, *Christ and the Common Life*, 51–198; more popularly, Amy Black, ed., *Five Views on the Church and Politics*, Counterpoints (Grand Rapids: Zondervan, 2015).

66. Note, e.g., the critiques of trends within the Black church in Marvin A. McMickle, *Where Have All the Prophets Gone? Reclaiming Prophetic Preaching in America* (Cleveland: Pilgrim, 2006), and Raphael G. Warnock, *The Divided Mind of the Black Church: Theology, Piety, and Public Witness* (New York: New York University Press, 2014).

67. Hauerwas, "Suffering Beauty," 151.

and with compassion. It must make evident that these virtues define who we *are* because this is who our God *is*.

With this orientation, these words of the psalmist make sense:

> LORD, who will sojourn in Your tent,
>   who will dwell on Your holy mountain?
> He who walks blameless
>   and does justice
>   and speaks the truth in his heart. (15:1–2)

> Who shall go up to the mount of the LORD,
>   and who will stand up in His holy place?
> The clean of hands and pure of heart,
>   who has given no oath in a lie,
>   and has sworn not in deceit. (24:3–4)

I close with these piercing, poetic words from Martin Luther King Jr. from his "Letter from a Birmingham Jail." In the midst of the crucible of the civil-rights era (1963) he wrote, "I have travelled the length and breadth of Alabama, Mississippi and all the other southern states. On sweltering summer days and crisp autumn mornings I have looked at her beautiful churches with their lofty spires pointing heavenward. I have beheld the impressive outlay of her massive religious buildings. Over and over again I have found myself asking: 'What kind of people worship here? Who is their God?'"[68]

---

68. Martin Luther King Jr., "Letter from a Birmingham Jail," in *I Have a Dream: Writings and Speeches That Changed the World*, ed. James Melvin Washington (New York: HarperSanFrancisco, 1992), 96.

4

Hope for the Future

The Relevance of Eschatology

The previous chapter ended with words from Martin Luther King Jr. This one begins with the final lines of a speech that he delivered at a church in Memphis (April 3, 1968). King was assassinated the next day.

> Well, I don't know what will happen now. We've got some difficult days ahead. But it doesn't matter with me now. Because I have been to the mountaintop. And I don't mind. Like anybody, I would like to live a long life. Longevity has its place. But I'm not concerned about that now. I just want to do God's will. And He's allowed me to go up to the mountain. And I've looked over. And I've seen the promised land. I may not get there with you. But I want you to know tonight, that we, as a people, will get to the promised land. And, I'm happy tonight. I'm not worried about anything. I'm not fearing any man. Mine eyes have seen the glory of the coming of the Lord.[1]

1. Martin Luther King Jr., "I See the Promised Land," in *I Have a Dream: Writings and Speeches That Changed the World*, ed. James M. Washington (New York: HarperCollins, 1992), 203.

These words communicate King's confidence in a changed world, a hope that had motivated him to persevere in the efforts to combat racism. It was a hope grounded in King's Christian faith and expressed eloquently in biblical imagery that gave significance to what he had accomplished in that long and difficult journey of reforming a nation. King's was a firm conviction that beyond the many personal trials of the civil rights movement; the ongoing legal conflicts at local, state, and national levels; and the inescapable broader upheavals accompanying needed societal change lay a world of justice and equality. Eschatology mattered.

It is not always so. Some Christian eschatological views major on particulars of chronology or other fine points of their proposed schemes, but the potential relevance for social and political life today is left unexplored or is tangential to their theological concerns.[2] Over the centuries, however, there have been significant instances where eschatology has been appropriated for the public square, for good and for ill.[3]

In recent decades some have contended that eschatology is key for understanding the mission of the church in the world. One example is Latin American liberation theology.[4] Start-

2. This is not true, of course, of all systems or theologians. Examples of theologians for whom eschatology is important are Jürgen Moltmann and Oliver O'Donovan. The profile mentioned here tends to be true of some evangelical persuasions. One theology textbook defines eschatology as "the study of last things, including Jesus' second coming, the resurrection, the final judgment, and the consummation." Michael F. Bird, *Evangelical Theology: A Biblical and Systematic Introduction*, 2nd ed. (Grand Rapids: Zondervan, 2020), 297. The Old Testament, however, conceives of a future new world order within history.

3. For a survey and taxonomy, see Jürgen Moltmann, *The Coming of God: Christian Eschatology*, trans. Margaret Kohl (Minneapolis: Fortress, 1996), 129–92 (he classifies these eschatological schemes as Messianic, Political, Ecclesiastical, or Epochal Millenarianism); Moltmann, *The Ethics of Hope*, trans. Margaret Kohl (Minneapolis: Fortress, 2012), 9–41 (the categories are Apocalyptic, Christological, Separatist, and Transformational Eschatology).

4. See, e.g., Ignacio Ellacuría, "Utopía y profetismo," in *Mysterium liberationis: Conceptos fundamentales de la teología de la liberación*, ed. Ignacio Ellacuría and Jon Sobrino, Colección Teología Latinoamericana 16 (San Salvador, El Salvador: UCA

ing with the conviction that the kingdom of God is already present in some form and rejecting its overspiritualization in certain church circles, liberation theologians advocate for the kingdom's ongoing realization today in concrete sociopolitical praxis aimed at creating a more just world. The partial human mediations of the kingdom generated by this praxis[5] inevitably oppose the status quo and so signal their demise while at the same time pointing to a future consummation of the kingdom when oppression will be no more. These theologians draw on the Marxist concept of utopia (particularly through the work of Ernst Bloch) but realign it with Christian faith. Liberation theology's eschatological vision reenforces its denunciation of current socioeconomic and political arrangements, which in God's future will be removed and then replaced.

An important early influence on the eschatology of Latin American liberation theology is *Theology of Hope* by the German theologian Jürgen Moltmann.[6] In his many publications he champions the importance of Christian hope for all kinds of social issues. Moltmann calls his view "transformative eschatology."[7] Liberation theology, while appreciative that Moltmann had brought eschatology into the center of theological discourse, criticizes him for not grasping deeply enough

Editores, 1991), 1:393–442; João Batista Libânio, "Esperanza, utopía, resurrección," in Ellacuría and Sobrino, *Mysterium liberationis*, 2:495–510; Gustavo Gutiérrez, *A Theology of Liberation: History, Politics and Salvation*, trans. Sister Caridad Inda and John Eagleson (Maryknoll, NY: Orbis Books, 1973), 160–68, 213–250; José Míguez Bonino, *Doing Theology in a Revolutionary Situation*, Confrontation Books (Philadelphia: Fortress, 1975), 132–53; Míguez Bonino, *Toward a Christian Political Ethics* (Philadelphia: Fortress, 1983), 87–94. For an exegetical example, see J. Severino Croatto on Isaiah in Daniel Patte, ed., *Global Bible Commentary* (Nashville: Abingdon, 2004), 195–211.

5. By this is meant the concrete sociopolitical and economic actions producing changes that approximate what are believed to be the ideals and demands of God's kingdom.

6. Jürgen Moltmann, *Theology of Hope: On the Ground and the Implications of a Christian Eschatology*, trans. James W. Leitch (New York: Harper & Row, 1975; German original, 1965).

7. Moltmann, *Ethics of Hope*, 35–41.

how terrible current conditions are the seedbed for hope and that actions today are not simply anticipations of the future but its actual manifestation in the here and now.[8]

Evangelicals of the Fraternidad Teológica Latinoamericana have been concerned, too, with contextualizing Christian hope to the realities of the Americas.[9] On the one hand, they are frustrated with the impact of more sensationalistic eschatological systems brought by certain mission groups. They see these as escapist and as discouraging more direct participation in societies that in the past were in the grips of civil war and that today continue to suffer extreme poverty, wrestle with the pervasive violence of drug cartels, and navigate the oppressive chaos of recent populist regimes. In the end, these theologians argue, this imported theology is conformist and fatalistic. Disengaged from the demands of Latin America, it is an ideological option (consciously or not) in support of maintaining (or ignoring) the existing state of affairs. On the other hand, they have sought to present what they believed to be a more biblical alternative to the utopian ideologies of Marxist movements and liberation theology.

Latino/a theologians in the United States turn to the concept of *mañana* ("tomorrow") to articulate an eschatology that can respond to the unique challenges of Latino/a communities.[10]

8. Gutiérrez, *Theology of Liberation*, 216–18; Míguez Bonino, *Doing Theology in a Revolutionary Situation*, 137–50; Míguez Bonino, "Reading Jürgen Moltmann from Latin America," *Asbury Theological Journal* 55, no. 1 (2000): 105–14. For Moltmann's response, see his *A Broad Place: An Autobiography*, trans. Margaret Kohl (Minneapolis: Fortress, 2008), 222–32.

9. E.g., Samuel Escobar, "El reino de Dios, la escatología y la ética social y política en América Latina," in *El reino de Dios y América Latina*, ed. C. René Padilla (El Paso: Casa Bautista de Publicaciones, 1975), 127–56; Alberto Fernando Roldán, *Escatología: Una visión integral desde América Latina* (Buenos Aires: Kairós, 2002), 115–86; Nelson R. Morales Fredes, "The Kingdom of God: Latin American Biblical Reflections on Eschatology," in *All Things New: Eschatology in the Majority World*, ed. Gene L. Green, Stephen T. Pardue, K. K. Yeo, Majority World Theology (Carlisle, UK: Langham Global Library, 2019), 85–104.

10. Justo L. González, *Mañana: Christian Theology from a Hispanic Perspective* (Nashville: Abingdon, 1990), 157–67; Luis G. Pedraja, *Teología: An Introduction to Hispanic Theology* (Nashville: Abingdon, 2003), 187–204; Oscar García-Johnson,

From this perspective, well-known expressions such as *mañana será otro día* ("tomorrow will be another day"), *siempre hay una mañana* ("there is always a tomorrow"), and *que será, será* ("whatever will be, will be") are not to be understood as a passive or defeatist acceptance of the ways things have been. Rather, they are statements expressing confidence that things will change in due time, so there needs to be fruitful engagement today with current social needs. This future is conceived not "in terms of continuity with a past filled with oppression, but rather as filled with a radical hope that the future will be transformed to bring justice, liberation, and life. Seeing that the present is not what it could be, our vision of *mañana*—of what could be, yet is not—serves as a constant judgment on the present. It is the radical questioning of the present as envisioned by God."[11] My purpose in citing these case studies briefly is neither to defend nor to evaluate them but rather to offer them as illustrative of eschatologies that are aware of the bearing of the future on the present. Each perceives eschatology as crucial for theological and ethical reflection and ecclesial participation in society. These examples range across geopolitical contexts (the United States, Latin America, and Western Europe) and theological persuasions. All of them couple sociopolitical, economic, and religious critique with visions of the possibilities of another tomorrow.

In the prophetic books we find a similar coordination of denunciation, judgment, and hope. In the past, many biblical scholars have bifurcated the prophets' messages of judgment from those of restoration, deeming them contradictory. This position rightly has been called into question. Their juxtaposition in prophetic books mirrors what we encounter in movements that strive for justice. Censure is fueled by a double eschatology: a soon-coming judgment to be followed by a fresh

---

The Mestizo/a Community of the Spirit: A Postmodern Latino/a Ecclesiology, Princeton Theological Monograph Series (Eugene, OR: Pickwick, 2009), 97–141.

11. Pedraja, *Teología*, 188.

work of God. While the previous two chapters explored the announcements of judgment on Israel, Judah, and the nations, this chapter concentrates on the prophetic hope of a new world of plenty, justice, and peace.

Some consider the prophetic passages about that future to be utopian literature. In that genre, utopias serve as critiques of the unacceptable inadequacies of society while also presenting an alternative world toward which a community can look in anticipation and attempt to approximate.[12] This approach resonates with the theological perspectives that I mentioned earlier. It is akin to Brueggemann's assertion that prophetic preaching of the prospect of another reality contradicts the reigning ideology and can galvanize the people of God to imagine life beyond the injustice that many take for granted and after the judgment that this must bring.[13]

The Hope for a Better Tomorrow

The prophets do not leave the community in despair, without expectation of anything more than suffering, loss, and ruins. With the demise of what was thought to be the natural order of things, for both the privileged and those who were its victims, the people of God would have had doubts about what might come next. Would there be anything beyond the collapse of their world? Was Yahweh capable of doing something new? Would Yahweh want to?

The prophets proclaim that God's commitment to them is deep and lasting, so even their harshest words always are followed by promises of restoration. The prophetic passion and

12. E.g., Ehud Ben Zvi, ed., *Utopia and Dystopia in Prophetic Literature* (Göttingen: Vandenhoeck & Ruprecht, 2006). This insight into prophetic literature arose within a context different from Latin American liberation theology's interest in utopia.

13. E.g., Walter Brueggemann, *The Prophetic Imagination*, 40th anniv. ed. (Minneapolis: Fortress, 2018); Brueggemann, *The Practice of Prophetic Imagination: Reality, Grief, Hope; Three Urgent Prophetic Tasks* (Grand Rapids: Eerdmans, 2014).

the divine demand for justice are inseparable from the pledge of renewal. In her introduction to a collection of essays by her father Abraham Heschel, Susannah Heschel captures this prophetic heartbeat: "The prophets know that unless we understand the very depths of corruption, misery, and despair, the hope we offer is superficial. Only the prophet who gives voice to the silent agony, who rages against injustice, whose passion exudes from every word, can offer true hope that 'evil is never the climax of history,' that redemption will come."[14] This future is important to the visions of Amos, Isaiah, and Micah. As we saw in the previous two chapters, these books herald imminent judgment on pride and the wrongs it fosters, but there is a second component of what God will do. They proclaim the hope of life in a revitalized world, a new social construction of reality where all will be made right. Judgment is not the end of Yahweh's work. It is the necessary step toward a more glorious reality, and that sublime future, like the judgment, was relevant for life in Israel and Judah.

My discussion of that brighter future is limited to a few passages that reflect three of its dimensions. The large number of passages in our prophetic books that deal with themes of hope, especially in Isaiah, requires that this presentation be selective, even as it is generally representative. The future that these passages portray is of a world of plenty, of a just ruler, and of relevant worship. These mirror the three features of Israel and Judah that the prophets condemn: socioeconomic oppression, corrupt and callous leadership, and deplorable worship.

A World of Peace and Abundance

A fundamental component of these three aspects of the future is that all of them are connected to the ancient context.

---

14. Susannah Heschel, "Reading Abraham Heschel Today," in *Thunder in the Soul: To Be Known by God*, ed. Robert Erlewine, Plough Spiritual Guides (Walden, NY: Plough, 2021), xx–xxi.

Each represents a striking reversal of what the prophets condemned. Consequently, this hope could be appropriated *for* life *then* and *there*. It did not serve some sort of escapist strategy designed to avoid the present. Instead, it offered a new perspective on the injustice the people were enduring and the ravages of the coming judgment. The promise was that a remnant, those who would return from exile and those who had remained and been faithful, would have a fresh start in the land.

I start with the short passage at the end of the book of Amos (9:11–15). These verses respond to the appalling conditions in the Northern Kingdom and the impact of God's judgment on Israel's injustice and national exceptionalism. The passage can be split into two parts: the first begins with "on that day" (9:11) and the second with "days are coming" (9:13). Previously, these phrases introduced oracles of judgment (2:16; 4:2; 8:3, 9, 11, 13); here they signal a very different kind of announcement.

In the future, the passage declares, there will be ample food and drink for all. This is a stark contrast to the lack of water and the hunger that most were experiencing (4:6–9), even as a privileged few drank to their hearts' content and consumed the best meat, oblivious to the suffering all around them (4:1; 6:4–6). In that day, *everyone* will enjoy abundance (9:13). What is more, rather than the destruction of the nation's fortresses, the humiliation of its armies, and the displacement of some of the population into exile, Israel will be securely planted in its land (9:14, 15). No longer would they be under constant attack by the surrounding nations (1:3–15) or overrun by a mighty invader (2:13–14; 3:11; 6:14). Edom, their historic enemy, and those other nations will be brought into relationship with Yahweh (9:12)! The prospect of peace for a people for whom the horrors of war were a regular experience would have been a wonder.

In that time of peace, they will plant vineyards and gardens, and this without fear of another debacle resulting in removal

> And they shall build houses and dwell in them
> and plant vineyards and eat their fruit.
> They shall not build for another to dwell
> and shall not plant for another to eat.
>
> Isaiah 65:21–22a

from their land. Because vineyards and gardens must be nurtured over time to bear their produce,[15] these words reinforce the vision of the long-term absence of military conflict. This would have been an idyllic picture for a largely agrarian society of peasant farmers whose crops and livelihood had been disrupted by blight (4:9) and ravaged by war. The prophet also foretells the repairing of ruins and the rebuilding of towns. Both rural and urban life would flourish in incredible ways.

This portrait of radically transformed national existence was a further indictment of the status quo. This future represented what national life should have been and was not, but one day would be because of the divine promise. Yahweh, who through the prophet had censured all that was wrong in Israelite society and rejected its worship, was the guarantor of this hope. The first-person verbs in 9:11–15 leave no doubt as to who would bring this to pass. The current king and his regime, with the reigning ideology and its vision of national life, have no claim on the future. Yahweh *your* God has spoken (9:15).

Isaiah 65:17–25 resonates in several ways with the Amos passage, but its description of the future is more extensive and poignant. It is not only that God's people will build homes and plant their vineyards in peace. There is the added note that they will do so without the threat of having others live in their homes and seize the fruit of their labors (65:21–22). This

15. Philip J. King and Lawrence E. Stager, *Life in Biblical Israel*, LAI (Louisville: Westminster John Knox, 2001), 98–101.

reflects what sometimes happened when defeated people were taken into exile: the conqueror would bring others to take over their homes and farms. This happened when Israel fell to the Assyrians in 722 BCE (2 Kings 17:24).

With the end of war comes longer life. No more would there be shrieks of grief and mourning for the dead (Isa. 65:19). Children would not suffer as victims of the violence of combat (and there would be many descendants!), the young men would not perish too young, and the elderly would live out their days without trouble (65:20). In a powerful turn of phrase, Yahweh proclaims that no more "will they bear children doomed to misfortune" (65:23 NIV).[16] This peaceable scene is enriched by predators not attacking vulnerable animals.[17] There will be no more hurt or destruction (65:25). National trauma will end.[18]

This amazing vision of an undisturbed world of thriving homes, farms, and families surely represents a "new heavens and a new earth" (65:17; cf. 66:22)! This is not the new heavens and new earth of Revelation 21, which appropriates that vocabulary for another, grander vision. Here there will be death, but only after long life in the land. In this future reality, the heavens and earth that had been called to witness God's indictment (1:2) are renewed. Only the Creator could accom-

16. Misfortune would entail war, as well as disease, starvation, high rates of infant mortality, or other causes. See Kristine Henricksen Garroway, *Growing Up in Ancient Israel: Children in Material Culture and Biblical Texts*, Archaeology and Biblical Studies 23 (Atlanta: SBL Press, 2018), 223–65; Carol Meyers, *Rediscovering Eve: Ancient Israelite Women in Context* (New York: Oxford University Press, 2013), 49–58, 97–102. Alter understands the Hebrew to read, "nor give birth in panic."

17. Note the allusion in Isa. 65:25 to the curse of the serpent in Eden (Gen. 3:14). There are several other allusions to Gen. 1–3 in this passage that strengthen the idea that this is a new world.

18. Trauma theory, a new field of Old Testament research, can provide new insights into these texts. See David G. Garber Jr., "Trauma Theory and Biblical Studies," *Currents in Biblical Research* 14, no. 1 (2016): 24–44; cf. Alphonso Groenewald, "'Trauma Is Suffering That Remains': The Contribution of Trauma Studies to Prophetic Studies," *Acta Theologica* 38, no. 26 (2018): 88–102.

plish this (cf. 42:5; 45:7, 12, 18, etc.),[19] and he rejoices over restored Jerusalem (65:18–19), that chosen city condemned in the first chapter of the book. Yahweh will be especially attentive to the people; the issues of the past will remain in the past (65:17; cf. 43:18). Their relationship with God will be fully restored. Indeed, all will become new (cf. 42:9; 43:19; 48:6–8; 62:2).

A Just Ruler

The dire situations in which Israel and Judah found themselves were due in large part to the decisions of immoral leadership. Hope for the future, then, included a political component. A different kind of ruler would be needed to lead the people in the restoration. Of our three books, Isaiah has the most material on kingship. This is due in part to its size, but the theme is central for that book in ways that it is not in Amos and Micah.[20]

Importantly, Isaiah is bracketed by two impressive revelations of Yahweh as king. The call of the prophet in chapter 6 pictures the divine king sitting on a "high and lofty throne" (v. 1). The book's final chapter begins with the cosmic king declaring, "The heavens are My throne and the earth is My footstool" (66:1). In addition, the kingship of God appears periodically throughout the book. As king, Yahweh brings charges against the people for their sin (41:21); he is their Creator (43:15) and

19. For a succinct discussion of the linking of Yahweh as Creator and Redeemer, especially in the prophetic literature, see Mark J. Boda, *The Heartbeat of Old Testament Theology: Three Credal Expressions* (Grand Rapids: Baker Academic, 2017), 90–95.

20. For God as king and for the future human king in Isaiah, see Andrew T. Abernethy, *The Book of Isaiah and God's Kingdom: A Thematic-Theological Approach*, New Studies in Biblical Theology (Downers Grove, IL: IVP Academic, 2016); cf. H. G. M. Williamson, *Variations on a Theme: King, Messiah and Servant in the Book of Isaiah*, Didsbury Lecture Series (Carlisle: Paternoster, 1998), 1–29. For Micah, one can point to 5:2 [MT 5:1]; cf. 2:12–13. Amos 9:11, I believe, alludes to the Davidic dynasty.

Redeemer (44:6). Yahweh is the unrivaled, omnipotent sovereign who directs history according to plans established long ago (14:27; 23:9; 44:24–28; 45:20–21).

In the vision of chapter 6, Yahweh is surrounded by winged beings who are ready to obey whatever the most holy,[21] all-powerful, divine commander of the armies might command (6:1–5; cf. 57:15). He is greater than one of Judah's most distinguished kings, Uzziah, who had just died (6:1). Yahweh lives, and his glory fills the earth. Yahweh is more powerful than the Assyrian king (10:5–19), who is called the "great king" by the Rabshakeh at the walls of Jerusalem (36:4, 13). The misplaced arrogance of this conqueror of nations (36:7–10, 18–20) would be exposed. The Assyrian king's armies would be miraculously defeated; his fate was sealed (37:36–38).[22] The empire of Babylon also would be crushed (13:2–22) and its king and his sons executed at God's hand (14:3–23). Only Yahweh reigns forever!

It is this incomparable Enthroned One who declares to Judah that they will have a righteous Davidic king in the future.[23] For my purposes, at least three things stand out about this king. First, every passage that describes this individual explicitly says that he will bring justice, and several mention that his will be a rule of peace (9:6–7 [MT 9:5–6]; 11:1–5; 16:5; 32:1). This king is God's response to the socioeconomic oppression

21. The most significant name for Yahweh in Isaiah is the "Holy One" of Israel (1:4; 5:19, 24; 10:17, 20; 12:6; 17:7; 29:19, 23 [of Jacob]; 30:11, 12, 15; 31:1; 37:23; 40:25; 41:14, 16, 20; 43:3, 14, 15; 45:11; 47:4; 48:17; 49:7 [2x]; 54:4, 5; 57:15; 60:9, 14).

22. Shawn Zelig Aster argues that Isa. 6 satirizes Assyrian imperial ideology regarding the king's power and universal reach and critiques the co-optation of Judah's elites by that propaganda (*Reflections of Empire in Isaiah 1–39: Responses to Assyrian Ideology*, ANEM 19 [Atlanta: SBL Press, 2017], 41–80).

23. A more extensive study of Yahweh's future agents in Isaiah would include the servant of chaps. 40–66. I concentrate here only on the coming king. For coordinating the servant with that king, see the commentaries and the sources in n. 20; cf. Richard L. Schultz, "The King in the Book of Isaiah," in *The Lord's Anointed: Interpretation of Old Testament Messianic Texts*, ed. Philip E. Satterthwaite, Richard S. Hess, and Gordon J. Wenham (Carlisle: Paternoster, 1995), 141–65.

in Israel and the corrosive self-indulgent lifestyles of the comfortable that it sustains. In addition, the peace this king will
establish would not be the imposed peace of a *pax Assyriaca*,
where a negotiated peace would last only as long as annual
tribute was paid to the empire and its dictates obeyed. That
would be a deceiving quiet borne in submission and under the
constant fear of imperial invasion for noncompliance. Justice
in every dimension of national life, however, will be the lasting foundation of the reign of Yahweh's future king and true
peace its effect.

Second, two passages that announce this ruler are placed
in close proximity to a portrayal of Judah's king, making the
differences in leadership quite clear. How dissimilar the future
Davidic king of Isaiah 9 and 11 will be to the feckless Ahaz
(chap. 7)![24] The biblical text depicts Ahaz as one who did not
do what was right in God's eyes and practiced idolatry (2 Kings
16:1–4). He crumbled before pressure by Israel and Aram (Syria)
and sought help from the Assyrians (2 Kings 16:5–9), while at
the same time feigning piety at the prophet Isaiah's challenge
to ask Yahweh for a sign (any sign!) in that hour of need (Isa.
7:10–12). Those negotiations with the Assyrians turned Judah
into a vassal state of the empire. Ahaz then prostituted worship at the temple in Jerusalem with ideas he had picked up
in Damascus, when he presented himself before the Assyrian
king to express gratitude for the empire's help and to affirm his
subordinate status (2 Kings 16:10–18). The policies of the kings
of Judah and the Northern Kingdom vis-à-vis Assyria would

24. The other king named in Isaiah is Hezekiah. There are parallels between the
prophet's interaction with him and with Ahaz. Jerusalem again is under attack (7:1–2;
36:1–2); the king is at the upper pool on the way to the Washer's Field (7:3; 36:2);
he is told not to fear (7:4; 37:6); and there is mention of a sign (7:10–17; 37:30–32;
38:7, 22). Although Hezekiah seeks Yahweh's help (37:14–20) and is healed of sick-
ness (chap. 38), the royal court is censured for trusting in Egypt (chaps. 30–31), and
Hezekiah eventually reveals his pride and callousness (chap. 39). Even this more
godly king fails.

bring distress and dark gloom, and the people would turn bitterly from Yahweh. Unlike that "former" time of misfortune, however, in the "latter" time of the coming king there will be light, rejoicing, and victory (Isa. 8:19–9:5 [MT 8:19–9:4]).[25]

The outstanding abilities and character of this king are the third point to be drawn from these passages. The extravagant epithets of Isaiah 9:6 [MT 9:5] underscore the excellence of this Davidic ruler, and the zeal of Yahweh ensures that his reign would be a reality (9:7 [MT 9:6]).[26] This child, this royal son,[27] who will assume the throne will rule as

- Wondrous counselor. The label *counselor* (*yôʿēṣ*; 1:26; 3:3; 19:11; 41:28) refers to someone who makes political decisions, a statesman. This ruler will be wise and not make the ill-advised decisions of the leaders of Judah and other nations.

- Mighty God (*ʾēl gibbôr*).[28] This king will act with the power of God in accordance with the divine will.

- Everlasting father (*ʾăbîʿad*). In the ancient Near East, the title *father* conveyed the care and protection that kings

25. There is disagreement over whether "former" and "latter" refer to individuals (Alter) or to a time period (CEB, ESV, NASB, NIV, NRSV). Our reading takes the second option. See the commentaries.

26. Some argue that the titles communicate that the child will have divine attributes and thus be human and divine. See, e.g., John N. Oswalt, *The Book of Isaiah: Chapters 1–39*, NICOT (Grand Rapids: Eerdmans, 1986), 245–48. Another view is that these attributes point beyond the child to Yahweh, whose agent he is (e.g., Abernethy, *Book of Isaiah*, 125–28). My view is that in context these are hyperbolic titles that emphasize the king's capacities and dependence on God. This does not negate their appropriation for the messianic hope that would be fulfilled in Jesus.

27. The term *son* also could allude to his identity as a royal child. It is used in ancient Near Eastern texts and in key Old Testament passages to refer to the enthronement of a king or to his unique status before the deity (cf. 2 Sam. 7:14–16; Pss. 2:7; 72:1).

28. This is the translation of almost all English versions. Alter has "divine warrior." He does not take *ʾēl* as pointing to God but as an "intensifier" underscoring the strength of the *gibbôr*, the warrior.

ideally would offer their people. This king and his descendants will live out this charge faithfully for a very long time (cf. 2 Sam. 7:13, 16, 24–26, 29; Ps. 89:29).

- Prince of peace (*śar-śālôm*). In a context of periodic warfare, this king will assure enduring peace for the nation and the world.

To this list of descriptors, 11:1–5 adds a set of divinely bestowed abilities. This king, this passage says, will arise from the stump of Jesse—that is, from the devastated Davidic monarchy. In the context of the passage, with Assyrian aggression looming, a viable political future seemed impossible (cf. 4:2; 6:13).[29] These divine endowments[30] appear in three pairs: wisdom and understanding, counsel and strength, and the knowledge and fear of God (11:2). That is, not only will this king be *competent* and *capable* to do what he must; he also will have the *character* to meet challenges with discernment, integrity, and obedience to Yahweh. He will be distinguished by the consistent fear of Yahweh, not a wavering devotion (11:3–5). These qualities will be on display in how he skillfully adjudicates conflicts without bias toward the powerful while keeping a protective eye on the vulnerable. He will be decisive with the wicked and rule with equity and righteousness. The absence of danger throughout his dominion is depicted in an astonishing scene

29. The picture may be of a stem that is sprouting, not that of a stump. Note the immediately preceding judgment on Assyria that is described as cutting down of trees (Isa. 10:33–34).

30. Scholars disagree on whether the reference is to Yahweh's Spirit (NIV, ESV) or to the power of God working in this person (NRSV, CEB; cf. 4:4; 28:5–6). The Spirit of Yahweh also will rest on the Servant (42:1; cf. 61:1). For a helpful discussion, see Hilary Marlow, "The Spirit of Yahweh in Isaiah 11:1–9," in *Presence, Power, and Promise: The Role of the Spirit of God in the Old Testament*, ed. David G. Firth and Paul D. Wegner (Downers Grove, IL: IVP Academic, 2011), 220–32. Individuals enabled by God's Spirit include the designers of the tabernacle (Exod. 31:1–5), judges (Judg. 3:10; 6:34; etc.), Saul (1 Sam. 10:10; etc.), and David (1 Sam. 16:13; 23:2; cf. Ps. 51:1 [MT 51:4]).

> And the spirit of the LORD shall rest on him,
>   a spirit of wisdom and insight,
> a spirit of counsel and valor,
>   a spirit of knowledge and fear of the LORD.
>
> Isaiah 11:2

that couples dangerous predators and poisonous snakes with weaker animals and little children. This peace will spread out from Jerusalem to encompass the entire world. The fact that the knowledge of God will fill the earth means that everything will function harmoniously (11:6–9). Creation is renewed and society regenerated to better ends (cf. 65:25). How radically different this will be from what the people had experienced under their kings. Instead of exploitation, there will be efficacious justice; instead of the never-ending dark clouds of war, a glorious peace!

This Davidic king, however, is not the only divinely empowered ruler in the book. Cyrus is called God's shepherd (44:28) and then surprisingly Yahweh's "anointed one" (45:1; literally, his "messiah"; *māšîaḥ*)! Indeed, Cyrus is selected and enabled to fulfill God's purpose to facilitate the return of his people to the land. However, twice the text says that Cyrus does not know Yahweh (45:4–5).[31] This is quite dissimilar to the portrait of the messianic Davidic king of 9:6–7 [MT 9:5–6] and 11:1–5, whose person is stamped with the very presence of Yahweh. Cyrus is chosen for a particular task at one moment in history and then passes away, whereas the presence and impact of the king of promise will stand.

The reversal of socioeconomic conditions and an end to armed conflict would require changed political realities. Ac-

---

31. Alter has "when I had not known you" in 45:4 and omits the second occurrence in 45:5.

cordingly, restoration to the land and abundance for all will be made sure by the presence of a Spirit-filled ruler whose reign will bring justice and peace. One aspect of the prophetic critique remains: unacceptable worship. How does the prophetic hope envision reversal in religious life?

Transformed Worship

Religious centers, rituals, and personnel are vigorously condemned in Amos, Isaiah, and Micah. Amos announces that Bethel, the key sanctuary of the Northern Kingdom, will be brought down (3:14; 9:1), and it is noteworthy that the vision at the end of the book does not include a temple (9:11–15). The prophet proclaims that Yahweh speaks from Zion and is not present at Israel's sanctuaries (1:2; 4:12); the future is connected to Judah (9:11). In other words, hope for acceptable religious life lies in the South. Isaiah 2:2–4 and Micah 4:1–3, which are strikingly similar,[32] envisage that profoundly changed religious reality. These verses depict the house of Yahweh on Zion as being lifted high above all else, establishing its unique importance (Isa. 2:2; Mic. 4:1).[33]

In a surprising twist, the nations will flow to Zion, streaming like a river (the verb *nāhar*) to the city, not to attack it but to come to the temple (Isa. 2:2–3). To "go up" to the mountain of Yahweh reflects pilgrimage language, but here it is other

32. For discussions of the relationship between the two passages, see the commentaries on Isaiah and Micah.

33. Zion plays a significant role in Isaiah and Micah. For comparative studies, see, e.g., Gary Stansell, *Micah and Isaiah: A Form and Tradition Historical Comparison*, SBL Dissertation Series 85 (Atlanta: Scholars Press, 1988), 39–66; Frederik Poulsen, *Representing Zion: Judgement and Salvation in the Old Testament*, Copenhagen International Seminar (London: Routledge, 2015); for Isaiah, Andrew T. Abernethy, *Discovering Isaiah: Content, Interpretation, Reception*, Discovering Biblical Texts (Grand Rapids: Eerdmans, 2021), 75–99; for Micah, Rick R. Marrs, "'Back to the Future': Zion in the Book of Micah," in *David and Zion: Biblical Studies in Honor of J. J. M. Roberts*, ed. Bernard F. Batto and Kathryn L. Roberts (Winona Lake, IN: Eisenbrauns, 2004), 77–96.

> And all the nations shall flow to it
> and many people shall go, and say:
> Come, let us go up to the mount of the LORD,
> to the house of Jacob's God,
> that He may teach us of His ways
> and that we may walk in His paths.
>
> Isaiah 2:2b–3a

peoples who make the trek to Jerusalem. They come to learn God's Torah, seeking instruction for life. In that day, this word of Yahweh will be shared with all nations. They will appreciate the wisdom and benefits of following in God's ways (cf. Isa. 51:4–5; 66:18–21; cf. Deut. 4:6–8; Gen. 12:1–3). They will act differently, particularly in relationship to international conflict, because Yahweh will resolve their disputes. The motivations and rationale for war will be eliminated. Nations of their own accord will melt down their weapons (swords and spears) to reshape them into farm tools (plowshares, pruning hooks), and they will not learn the bloody art of war anymore.[34] This is a pointed contradiction to the plans for defense against the Assyrian attack by Ahaz and Hezekiah, as they depended on their politics and armor to stem the tides of war (e.g., Isa. 2:7; 7:1–9; 30:1–5, 7, 15–17; 31:1–3; 36:1–2; 39:2).

This truly amazing vision is even more striking because of where these passages occur in Isaiah and Micah. In both cases, the present state of Zion is described in the preceding verses. In Isaiah 1, Jerusalem is likened to Sodom and Gomorrah (v. 9) and a whore (v. 21). The once faithful city is full of corruption

---

34. The reality was often the reverse: turning farm implements into weapons because of the need to conscript ordinary citizens for war (1 Sam. 13:19–21). Joel 3:9–12 [MT 4:9–12] appears to contradict the language of this verse, but see Hans Walter Wolff, "Swords into Plowshares: Misuse of a Word of Prophecy?," *Currents in Theology and Mission* 12, no. 3 (1985): 133–47.

(vv. 23–31), and every worship activity on Yahweh's holy mountain is repugnant because the people legitimate, or at the very least ignore, injustice and violence (vv. 10–21). It is a false deity whom the people adore, and Yahweh will have none of it. In that day, through judgment, Yahweh will purify and restore Zion to righteousness and faithfulness (vv. 26–27). Judah and its capital, which have become God's enemy (v. 24), will now be the place to which nations will come to learn how to follow Yahweh. If current worship triggers divine reproach, in the future Zion and the temple will welcome the world. The juxtaposition of this passage in chapter 2 concerning future Zion with the extensive diatribe in chapter 1 against the current practices on Zion highlights the positive global impact of transformed worship. The cessation of war will signify that the time of those rejected rituals and God's judgment on them and Jerusalem will have passed.

The corresponding passage in Micah (4:1–3) also follows the condemnation of religious activity on Zion (3:5–12). While both Isaiah 1 and these verses in Micah mention judges and other leaders, only Micah refers to prophets and priests and their shameless participation in the injustice and corruption. It may not be a coincidence that religious personnel have no part in the dissemination of God's Torah from Zion. Those supposed gatekeepers of Yahweh's truth will be set aside. Worship in Yahweh's dwelling place on Zion then will be acceptable to God and a testimony to all.

An additional item appears in Micah 4:4. The peacefulness is described as each person's property and its yield being secure (cf. Deut. 8:7–10; 1 Kings 4:25 [MT 5:5]). In this wondrous vignette, no one will cause the people to "tremble." This verb (*ḥrd*, hiphil) can be used of panic before an enemy (e.g., Lev. 26:6; Judg. 8:12; 2 Sam. 17:2; Ezek. 30:9). Having no fear is a fitting corollary to the elimination of the weapons of war. Importantly, it is Yahweh of the armies who assures that this promise is trustworthy. He has the authority and power to

> And they shall dwell each man beneath his vine
> and beneath his fig tree, with none to make him
>   tremble,
> for the mouth of the LORD of Armies has
>   spoken.
>
>   Micah 4:4

maintain that new world order. These words of agricultural bliss did not come from the Assyrian Rabshakeh, who used the same image as imperial rhetoric to press Jerusalem to surrender and to entrust themselves to the largesse of the empire and so avoid the slaughter of a siege (Isa. 36:16–17; cf. 2 Kings 18:31–32).

These two hope passages close with responses of commitment that play off what is said by the nations. Their "come, . . . that we may walk" (Isa. 2:3) is echoed by the people of God's "come, let us walk" (Isa. 2:5) and "we shall walk" (Mic. 4:5). In the former, the exhortation is to walk in the light of Yahweh, and in the latter, to walk in the name of Yahweh "our God" forever and ever. Light is a significant theme in Isaiah. Its mention brings to mind the light that will accompany the coming king (9:2 [MT 9:1]) and the glories of God's restorative actions (e.g., 30:26; 42:16; 51:4; 58:8; 60:1). In context, to walk in this light is to observe God's directives in worship and life and to seek the prophesied peace. In Micah, although other nations claim to want to walk in Yahweh's paths (4:3), ultimately they will walk in the name of their gods—not so Yahweh's people (4:5). In a fashion similar to the line in Isaiah, to walk in Yahweh's name is to follow what God lays out in Micah 4:1–3, with different worship and life emanating from Zion.

These two pledges are worthy replies to what God will do, but there also are words of consolation in Isaiah to encourage the people to embrace in faith the promises of another future. In times of trouble there had been cries of lament (Mic. 1:8, 16), because the people felt that Yahweh had turned his back and abandoned them (Isa. 40:27; 49:14; 63:15; 64:7, 12 [MT 64:6, 11]). Yet the prophetic word emphasizes that Yahweh has not forgotten them (Isa. 49:15–16; Mic. 7:18–20). In trusting him they will find comfort (Isa. 12:1; 40:1; 49:13; 51:3, 12, 19; 52:9; 54:11; 57:18; 61:2; 66:13) and renew their strength (40:6–8, 28–31). The calls to respond to Yahweh and his plans include

- *Do not fear*, because Yahweh is with you (Isa. 7:4; 8:12; 35:4; 37:6–7; 41:10, 13–14; 43:1; 44:2, 8; 51:7; 54:4, 14).
- *Rejoice* in the future that Yahweh will establish (Isa. 9:3; 12:3; 25:9; 35:1–2; 41:16; 61:7, 10; 65:13, 18; 66:10, 14), even as God will rejoice over his people and Zion (62:5; 65:19)!
- *Sing* praises to Yahweh for this glorious restoration (Isa. 12:5–6; 23:16; 24:14; 26:19; 27:2; 35:6; 42:10–11; 44:23; 49:13; 52:8; 54:1; 65:14), for in that day even nature will sing (55:12).
- An impressive series of exhortations found in Isaiah 51: "listen to me," "look" (v. 1); "look" (v. 2); "hearken to Me" (v. 4); "lift up your eyes" (v. 6); "listen to Me," "do

He gives vigor to the weary,
    and great power to those sapped of strength.
. . . .
But who wait for the LORD shall renew vigor,
    shall grow new pinions like the eagles,
shall run and shall not tire,
    walk on and not be weary.

Isaiah 40:29, 31

not be afraid" (v. 7); "awake, awake," "awake" (v. 9); and
"awake, awake, rise up" (v. 17).

Yahweh beckons. Those who live according to God's will and in
anticipation of participating in the fulfillment of the promises
will be called Yahweh's servants (54:17; 63:17; 65:8, 9, 13–15;
66:14).

In sum, the hope offered by Amos, Isaiah, and Micah is wide-
ranging. This prophetic imagination concerning the future depicts a time of plenty and peace under the rule of a divinely
empowered king, who will establish justice in the land and
elsewhere. Societies will be changed. In that day, too, a proper
relationship with Yahweh will be reflected in transformed worship on a renewed Zion that will stand as a beacon of righteousness to the world.

This is not a vision cast without expectations for those who
receive it. Trust in the faithfulness and power of Yahweh, celebration at the announcement of the dawning of the new age,
and obedience pursued in the expectancy of that coming kingdom were the markers of faith that these prophetic messages
seek. Hope was to be taken to heart and lived out in society
and in history. Eschatology mattered.

Prophetic Hope for Today

Across the centuries, humanity has yearned for a different reality in which there would be justice in the courts and in the
marketplace; where people of integrity serve in public office;
where everyone might have meaningful work, raise their children without fear, and aspire with confidence to achieve a level
of happiness and success. This shared human hope inescapably
contradicts the realities of every society and nation.

In the firm conviction that the Lord of history can bring
new life, restoring what has been marred by sin and judgment,

the books of Amos, Isaiah, and Micah offer remarkable pictures of renewal for the people of God and the world. If the prophetic imagination removes the veil over our eyes concerning the ugliness of injustice and the destructive arrogance of political actors and nation-states, while also exposing the lies of the ideologies that defend all of that, it also directs our attention to another world that lies beyond the suffering of today and beyond the judgment on that unacceptable state of affairs. To add another layer to individual and collective guilt, the perversity of compromising the worship of our God to sustain deplorable sociopolitical and economic constructs is an affront to the Christian faith, a sad testament to the health of the church, and more importantly, an offense to the person of God. This, too, will end.

The hope presented by these prophetic books is as broad as the transgressions they condemn. They speak of an era of justice, abundance, sanctified leadership, peace, and proper worship to be established by God for the benefit of the people of God and all nations, to his glory. This powerful prophetic imagination comes with calls to have faith in the trustworthiness and power of the person of Yahweh to accomplish that vision. This faith involves the exhortation to walk in the ways of God—that is, to live in accordance with the divine will in the conviction (and joy!) that these promises will come to pass. The social imaginaries of our societies (and sadly, often our theologies) cannot fathom or even allow the vision of a different world. The prophets, though, announce not only that these structures cannot continue but that they *will not*.

It is not surprising that several of the passages considered in this chapter have prompted serious reflection on possibilities of change. A few examples will suffice. In the aftermath of the long civil war in Guatemala (1960–96), the counterimages in Amos 9:11–15 of rebuilding ruins and of plenty could encourage readers to reimagine national reconstruction and consider the church's participation in rebuilding peace and prosperity in that Central American country.[35] On December 10, 1964, Martin Luther King Jr. incorporated the imagery of Isaiah 2 and Micah 4 into his acceptance speech for the Nobel Peace Prize to once again paint a picture of a country where justice finally would prevail:

> I believe that wounded justice, lying prostrate on the blood-flowing streets of our nations, can be lifted from this dust of shame to reign supreme among the children of men. . . . I still believe that one day mankind will bow before the altars of God and be crowned triumphant over war and bloodshed, and nonviolent redemptive good will proclaim the rule of the land. "And the lion and the lamb shall lie down together and every man shall sit under his own vine and fig tree and none shall be afraid." I still believe that we shall overcome![36]

A volume titled *Isaiah's Vision of Peace in Biblical and Modern International Relations* brings together papers from a 2005 international conference in Florence, Italy, that explore the ongoing relevance of Isaiah 2:1–5 for contemporary politics.[37]

35. M. Daniel Carroll R., "Reflecting on War and Utopia in the Book of Amos: The Relevance of a Literary Reading of the Prophetic Text from Central America," in *The Bible in Human Society: Essays in Honour of John W. Rogerson*, ed. D. J. A. Clines, P. R. Davies, and M. D. Carroll R., JSOTSup 200 (Sheffield: Sheffield Academic, 1995), 105–21; Carroll R., "Living between the Lines: A Reading of Amos 9:11–15 in Postwar Guatemala," *Religion & Theology* 6, no. 1 (1999): 50–64.

36. Martin Luther King Jr., "Nobel Prize Acceptance Speech," in King, *I Have a Dream*, 110–11.

37. Raymond Cohen and Raymond Westbrook, eds., *Isaiah's Vision of Peace in Biblical and Modern International Relations: Swords into Plowshares*, Culture and Religion in International Relations (New York: Palgrave Macmillan, 2008). Not all agree with this appreciation of Isa. 2. See J. J. M. Roberts, "The End of War in the Zion Tradition: The Imperialistic Background of an Old Testament Vision of Worldwide Peace," in *Character Ethics and the Old Testament: Moral Dimensions of Scripture*, ed. M. Daniel Carroll R. and Jacqueline Lapsley (Louisville: Westminster John Knox, 2007), 119–28. For a biblical commentary on Mic. 4:1–5 and its importance for peace, see Daniel L. Smith-Christopher, *Micah*, Old Testament Library (Louisville: Westminster John Knox, 2015), 139–45.

Each major section of the compendium matches a biblical or an ancient Near Eastern scholar with someone from the field of international relations. In another publication Latino Old Testament scholar Gregory Lee Cuéllar puts the diaspora experiences and hopes for return in Isaiah 40–55 into dialogue with those of the Mexican diaspora community in the United States.[38] This exercise illumines both the text and its immigrant readers, even as it provides the latter with a more profound sense of identity and a deeper understanding of the complexities of their marginalization in relation to their faith. The rhetoric of Isaiah, he argues, finds a counterpart in the Mexican immigrant *corridos*. With poignancy, these popular ballads sing of the difficulties of the journey north and of life in this country and the yearning for home. One could cite myriad other instances of the appropriation of these hope passages of our prophetic books throughout history, as well as those announcing a coming king that have been utilized in messianic movements of all kinds.

The point is that these texts continue to impact how the people of God struggle with how to approach societal transformation and wrestle with its relationship to their theology, worship practices, and Christian mission. As in the case of the denunciation described in the preceding chapters, this hope component of the prophetic imagination does not provide action steps. These visions of the future reinforce prophetic censure by contrasting what is with what one day will be. They underscore that what is unacceptable is not permanent, no matter how impossible that might seem. In this the people of God should find comfort and confidence, rejoicing in that reality that lies ahead. Each believer and each community of faith have the obligation to ponder in their own sociohistorical

38. Gregory Lee Cuéllar, *Voices of Marginality: Exile and Return in Second Isaiah 40–55 and the Mexican Immigrant Experience*, American University Series 7: Theology and Religion 271 (New York: Peter Lang, 2008).

contexts and in accordance with the avenues of action available
to them what it means to walk in the light and name of Yahweh
in tangible ways that are commensurate with this vision of the
future.[39] These texts do not contemplate passive readers. Only if
we inhabit the exhortations of these promises can those around
us desire to learn God's ways and see a better path forward
instead of being witnesses of the Christian church's ongoing,
deep moral and ideological failures.

39. For example, how might the passages of peace and a peaceful Messiah inform
action today? Another component can be the theological tradition within which the
individual or community is located, which can define the nature of the relationship
between church and society for its adherents.

Epilogue

Toward the Prophetic Vision for Today

The prophetic imagination is expansive. Our survey of the visions of the present and the future in the books of Amos, Isaiah, and Micah reveals how broad was their engagement with social life. They hit hard against injustice and with shocking rhetoric expose its cruelty and violence. These texts denounce the arrogance of political leaders and the misplaced confidence of national exceptionalism. They denounce in no uncertain terms the worship of an idol called Yahweh that had been crafted to sustain the reigning ideologies that wove their destructive lies into the hearts and minds of nations, even of the people of God. The prophetic literature declares that there will come a moment when God must judge the individuals and structures that perpetuate so much evil. This is the lens into reality revealed by the prophetic imagination: harsh realism charged with unwavering honesty about the world.

But the prophetic imagination offers more. Justice ultimately requires judgment, but those times of judgment do not foreclose history's horizons or define without remainder the person of Yahweh. No, one day all that is wrong will be made right:

scarcity will be no more, international relations will be characterized by peace, and a Spirit-filled ruler will transform political life. Then, Yahweh will be worshiped properly, and humanity will confess that Yahweh is the Holy and Compassionate One, the only God. Prophetic censure and the declarations of judgment and hope were all intertwined with current social life.

Throughout history that prophetic imagination has spawned multiple ecclesial and social movements. These texts have moved beyond their historical moorings and, as Scripture, continue to present an enduring message that reshapes how Christians view the church and the world and live life. The prophetic literature disrupts our constructions of reality, subverting the social imaginaries that mold us into unquestioningly absorbing destructive ideologies and values that sanction violence and leave victims in their wake. It is disconcerting to see how many Christians, churches, and institutions avoid these uncomfortable words or, even worse, participate in the very sins that the prophets denounce. They support political agendas, knowingly or blindly, of the Left or the Right in the words that are preached, the songs that are sung, the conferences that are organized, and the books that are published. God has been co-opted and the prophetic voice ignored or twisted. The wondrous hope that the prophetic texts announce, which should serve to further condemn the status quo, is limited in some theological circles to debates about chronological frameworks; in others, they are spiritualized to such an extent that their potential to empower the downtrodden and spur transformation is lost.

For Christians, there can be no greater motivation to live and speak prophetically than to look at the life and ministry of Jesus. He appealed to the prophetic literature in his ethical teaching,[1] but more importantly, he embodied prophetic

1. For accessible discussions of the relevance of the Old Testament for Jesus's ethics and the New Testament, see John Goldingay, *Do We Need the New Testament? Letting the Old Testament Speak for Itself* (Downers Grove, IL: IVP Academic,

ministry. Among his various roles, Jesus was a prophet, the greatest prophet.[2]

To begin with, the *message* of Jesus is prophetic. The woes of Matthew 23 echo prophetic concerns and intensity. Jesus is blistering in his critique of hypocritical religious practices and of religious leaders. He is not afraid to speak out against the political establishment and, in light of the coming judgment on Jerusalem and the temple, urges the people to turn to God. His *ministry* is prophetic. Jesus was sent by God, and he performs miraculous deeds. Jesus is recognized as a prophet by the masses (Luke 7:16–17; 9:18–19), the disciples (24:18–21; cf. Acts. 3:22–23), and his enemies (Luke 9:7–9; 22:63–65).

Jesus was like Jeremiah (Jer. 7:1–11), denouncing unacceptable worship in the temple (Luke 19:45–48). Like Elijah (1 Kings 17:17–24) and Elisha (2 Kings 4:32–37), he raised a widow's son (Luke 7:11–17).[3] At the synagogue in Nazareth Jesus combined two prophetic passages (Isa. 61:1–2a; 58:6) to define his ministry and then reprimanded the townspeople's pushback with examples from the lives of Elijah and Elisha (Luke 4:16–30). At the transfiguration, Jesus appeared with Moses and Elijah

---

2015), 139–56; Goldingay, *Reading Jesus's Bible: How the New Testament Helps Us Understand the Old Testament* (Grand Rapids: Eerdmans, 2017), 208–47; Ellen Davis, *Biblical Prophecy: Perspectives for Christian Theology, Discipleship, and Ministry*, Int (Louisville: Westminster John Knox, 2014), 207–40; David P. Gushee and Glen H. Stassen, *Kingdom Ethics: Following Jesus in Contemporary Context*, 2nd ed. (Grand Rapids: Eerdmans, 2016), 3–10, 22–24 passim.

2. See, e.g., N. T. Wright, *Jesus and the Victory of God*, Christian Origins and the Question of God 2 (Minneapolis: Fortress, 1996), 147–97; James D. G. Dunn, *Jesus Remembered*, Christianity in the Making 1 (Grand Rapids: Eerdmans, 2003), 655–67; cf. Walter Brueggemann, *The Prophetic Imagination*, 40th anniv. ed. (Minneapolis: Fortress, 2018), 81–113. I limit my attention primarily to the Gospel of Luke, although there are parallels in the other Gospels. For Luke, note Darrell L. Bock, *A Theology of Luke and Acts*, Biblical Theology of the New Testament (Grand Rapids: Zondervan, 2012), 189–93. Of course, there is much more that one could explore in connection with the person and ministry of Jesus and with the rest of the New Testament. Our engagement is limited and more focused.

3. Perhaps in an appeal to the Elijah connection (1 Kings 18:38), his disciples ask him to call fire down from heaven on a Samaritan village (Luke 9:51–55).

> The Spirit of the Lord is on me,
>   because he has anointed me
>   to proclaim good news to the poor.
> He has sent me to proclaim freedom for the
>   prisoners
>   and recovery of sight for the blind,
> to set the oppressed free,
>   to proclaim the year of the Lord's favor.
>
> Luke 4:18–19 NIV

(Luke 9:28–36). A voice from heaven told Peter, James, and John to listen to Jesus, much like in the Old Testament, where the people were commanded to pay attention to the prophets.

Clearly, Jesus saw himself as a prophet, and his hearers did too. In the end, Jesus suffered the fate of a prophet (Luke 13:33–35). He was continually opposed by other voices, rejected by his own people, paraded through a mockery of justice with the complicity of the religious establishment, and crucified by the Roman Empire. Jesus communicated a message and acted in ways consistent with the prophets of centuries past. In his resurrection he certified that hope in the restoration and redemption of life had birthed its firstfruits. The prophetic imagination lived on in and through Jesus.

The mantle of prophetic imagination has passed on to his people. The urgency to communicate it has increased because Jesus, the long-awaited king who would rule in the Spirit has come, and the kingdom of which the prophets spoke has been inaugurated, although not in its fullness. We live in that in-between time until his second coming. Until that day, the books of Amos, Isaiah, and Micah remain texts that challenge unjust dominant socioeconomic and political structures and actors and condemn co-opted religion masquerading as Christian faith. Their words will be resisted and the possibility of the end of our social imaginary doubted. In the face of compromises and reservations, our first task is to convince the people of God that today's ideologies that hold us in their grip are untenable and that judgment is both necessary and certain. At the same time, there is the further task of helping God's people embrace the truth of a new reality, anticipated in the resurrection of Jesus. Both components of the prophetic imagination—critique and hope—demand a different orientation to life in the world.

The theologies and movements that appeal to the prophetic literature, which I have mentioned in this volume, at some point also appeal to the person and words of Jesus to exhort their audience to participate in change. I will not survey those discussions here. Instead, I close with a call to consider this prophetic imagination as central to ecclesial mission. For this, I turn to Walter Moberly's discussion of the church as a plausibility structure.[4] Drawing on the work of missiologist Lesslie Newbigin, Moberly explains that the church is a plausibility structure in that it is a sociocultural context in which a set of beliefs, rooted in the Bible and history, are inculcated and incarnated in such a way that Christian beliefs and practices are believable both within the church and in the public square. He makes the telling observation: "The Bible is likely to be recognized as the privileged witness to God and the world only so far as living Christian witness attests at least somewhat persuasively to the truth of biblical content."[5]

What Moberly says about the Bible in general holds true for the prophetic imagination. If we do not inhabit it well and proclaim it with true integrity to a troubled church and a flawed

---

4. R. W. L. Moberly, *The Bible in a Disenchanted Age: The Enduring Possibility of Christian Faith*, Theological Explorations of the Church Catholic (Grand Rapids: Baker Academic, 2018), 99–109; cf. Leslie Newbigin, *The Gospel in a Pluralist Society* (Grand Rapids: Eerdmans, 1989), 8–9, 222–35.

5. Moberly, *Bible in a Disenchanted Age*, 102.

world, Christian Scripture and its revelatory potential about modern realities will be suspect. In fact, the Christian faith itself will be set aside as irrelevant and less than trustworthy. We are witnessing such a sea change in the culture today. Because of this, the prophetic imagination must be taken as integral to ecclesial mission. Only as we declare this vision and perform it faithfully among ourselves, before our neighbors, and within society, and only as we worship properly so that the true God might be known and made known, will the church live in a way worthy of its calling.

We can do no less.

Author Index

119

Scripture Index

Subject Index